Faith Seeking Assurance

SERIES EDITORS

Joel R. Beeke & Jay T. Collier

Interest in the Puritans continues to grow, but many people find the reading of these giants of the faith a bit unnerving. This series seeks to overcome that barrier by presenting Puritan books that are convenient in size and unintimidating in length. Each book is carefully edited with modern readers in mind, smoothing out difficult language of a bygone era while retaining the meaning of the original authors. Books for the series are thoughtfully selected to provide some of the best counsel on important subjects that people continue to wrestle with today.

Faith Seeking Assurance

Anthony Burgess

Edited by
Joel R. Beeke

Reformation Heritage Books
Grand Rapids, Michigan

Reformation Heritage Books
2965 Leonard St. NE
Grand Rapids, MI 49525
616-977-0889 / Fax 616-285-3246
orders@heritagebooks.org
www.heritagebooks.org

Printed in the United States of America
15 16 17 18 19 20/10 9 8 7 6 5 4 3 2 1

Library of Congress Control Number: 2015930233

For additional Reformed literature, request a free book list from Reformation Heritage Books at the above regular or e-mail address.

Table of Contents

Preface

Perhaps the most popular Scripture verse in contemporary culture is, "Judge not, that ye be not judged" (Matt. 7:1). We live in a time when tolerance reigns. Secular psychologists labor to relieve men, women, and children of their bad feelings about themselves. Churches proclaim God's unconditional love and teach that our duty is to learn to love ourselves. Schools instill in their students an ethic of acceptance of all people regardless of who they are and what they do. One would think that in such an environment, we would live in an age of great joy and peace.

Why then are we so restless and troubled?

It's not just secular or irreligious people. Many professing Christians suffer from a lack of joy and peace in their lives. Even if they denounce all forms of legalism and sing of the love of Christ, they still feel guilty and uneasy about themselves.

A major reason for this anxiety is a lack of spiritual assurance. The Holy Spirit alone can produce an inward confidence that you belong to Christ and Christ belongs to you, resulting in spiritual joy, peace, humility, love, longing for His presence, and desire to do His will. Spiritual assurance is not just a belief that you will be in heaven; it is heaven already begun in you. It is relying on what Christ did for you two thousand years ago and realizing what Christ is doing in your life today. Such assurance is not common.

You may think this is a strange idea, given that assurance of salvation is often said to be as easy as asking Jesus into your heart. Millions of people who pray such a prayer have been assured that they are children of God, forgiven of all their sins, and on the high road to heaven. Yet large numbers of them lack a heartfelt assurance. They have little motivation to serve the Lord and may drift in and out of churches.

Other Christians, of course, are in the opposite situation. They are the core of the churches' volunteers, or perhaps the pastors and paid staff. They believe that Christ died for sinners, read their Bibles, say their prayers, give their tithes and offerings to the church, and work hard to keep the Ten Commandments. They hate sin, love Christ, pursue holiness, and long to please and glorify God. Yet they may sometimes fear that God is angry with them and never feel truly accepted by the Lord. They seem to think it is almost impossible to know if they are children of God—a privilege reserved for the most saintly of saints.

Is it possible to experience assurance in the heart? If so, then how?

I have found tremendous help in answering these questions in the biblical teachings of a man born four hundred years ago. Anthony Burgess was the son of a schoolteacher born in Watford, Hertfordshire, England. He was educated at St. John's College, Cambridge (BA 1627), and Emmanuel College (MA 1630). He served as a fellow (instructor) at Emmanuel before becoming the vicar at Sutton Coldfield, Warwickshire, in 1635. During the English Civil War, he took refuge in Coventry and then was summoned to serve in the Westminster Assembly. His reputation grew as a godly man, a gifted preacher, and a profound theologian. After the war, he returned in 1647 to Sutton Coldfield, where he served until being expelled from his ministry in 1662 by the Act of Uniformity. He chose to retire to Tamworth, Staffordshire, and attended the parish church of his godly friend Samuel Langley until his death in 1664.

Burgess wrote many books, including major treatises on original sin, justification by faith alone, Christ's prayer in John 17,[1] and the goodness and functions of

---

1. For a summary of his treatise on John 17, see Joel R. Beeke, "Anthony Burgess on Christ's Prayer for Us," in *Taking Hold of God: Reformed and Puritan Perspectives on Prayer*, ed. Joel R. Beeke and Brian G. Najapfour (Grand Rapids: Reformation Heritage Books, 2011), 83–108.

the law of God.[2] Burgess's works were not reprinted in the nineteenth century, and, as a result, he is not as well known today as other Puritans like John Owen.

This book was adapted from Burgess's master-piece on assurance, *Spiritual Refining*, first published in London in 1652. I have spent over forty years reading books written in the seventeenth century, and this is one of my favorites.[3] The original book contained 120 sermons explaining, as the title page says, "the doctrine of assurance, the use of signs in self-examination, how true graces may be distinguished from counterfeit, several true signs of grace, and many false ones, the nature of grace under diverse Scripture notion or titles, as regeneration, the new creature, the heart of flesh, vocation, sanctification, etc."

The modern book that you hold in your hands takes the beginning (sermons 1–11) and an excerpt from the end (sermons 116–118) of the original volume. The resulting fourteen chapters give you the heart of Burgess's teaching in a manner that is short, simple, and sweet. You will find the pages full of the Holy Scriptures, for the Word of God is the only solid basis on

---

2. The last of these was recently reprinted as Anthony Burgess, *Vindiciae Legis*, Westminster Assembly Facsimile Series (Grand Rapids: Reformation Heritage Books, 2011).

3. For an analysis of Burgess's treatise on assurance, see Joel R. Beeke, "Anthony Burgess on Assurance," in *Puritan Reformed Spirituality* (Darlington, England: Evangelical Press, 2006), 170–95.

which we can build assurance. I encourage you to read it with an open Bible. Yet, since assurance is a gift of the Holy Spirit, I also encourage you to read this book with much prayer for the Father to work in you by the Spirit.

May the Lord be pleased to use this little book to do for you what the apostle John aimed to do in his first epistle: "These things have I written unto you that believe on the name of the Son of God; that ye may know that ye have eternal life" (1 John 5:13).

—Joel R. Beeke

CHAPTER 1

The Necessity and Advantage of Assurance

*Examine yourselves, whether ye be in
the faith; prove your own selves.*
—2 Corinthians 13:5

The church of Corinth was a garden planted by apostles, yet it was quickly filled with harmful weeds. The apostle Paul thus threatened the congregation with severe discipline if it failed to repent, ecclesiastical discipline being to the church what the sword is to the Commonwealth. The Corinthians did not care for this strong reprimand and responded by questioning Paul's apostolic power and authority. Love for their lusts and for security in those lusts made the Corinthians question the divine right of Christ's institutions. The apostle proved his calling by citing the spiritual success and powerful effect that his words had had among the Corinthians. Instead of proving and examining him, Paul commanded them to try themselves. This very argument may still be used

today by God's faithful ministers against many people
who condemn their calling.

The Duty to Examine Yourselves

In Paul's words there is a duty demanded. If this duty
is neglected, the consequences may be grave. The duty
is explained by two emphatic words: *examine* and *prove*
yourselves. The former word generally means to expe-
rientially know something that is uncertain, unknown,
or hidden. Knowledge gained by general arguments
and abstract reasons cannot be called experiential
knowledge. Therefore, in addition to this knowledge,
examination is needed to determine whether an end is
good or bad.

In an ill sense the word applies to the devil and his
instruments, while in a good sense it applies to God
and, in the text, to ourselves. In addition, these words
imply that men are strangers to themselves because
much self-love blinds them to the truth. These words
also imply that certain marks and signs indicate how
a man may come to certainty about who he is, or this
command would be in vain. The word *prove* also implies
that severe and diligent self-examination is necessary to
have a full experiential knowledge of what is within us
(Rom. 5:4).

The word *examine* is used in regard to experiential
knowledge. The object of examination is to see "whether
ye be in the faith." The apostle does not speak here of

the doctrine of faith, but of the saving grace of faith that is evident in the question, "Know ye not that Christ is in you?" The apostle says "ye in the faith" rather than "faith in you" to show the great extent of faith which we as its subjects cannot fully embrace. Additionally, he uses contrary phrases such as "in sin" and "in the flesh" rather than saying that sin and flesh are in us. Some also note that Paul says, "Enter thou into thy Master's joy," rather than "Thy Master's joy enter into thee"; though that seems fanciful, for the true meaning is, "Enter into the place of thy Master's joy" as the term is used in Esther.

Roman Catholic commentators elude this issue when asked by the orthodox to prove that a man may be certain of true grace in himself. They say the apostle does not refer to the saving work of the Spirit here, but of miraculous works. They argue that they are apostles of the true Messiah because of the miracles wrought among them. They also cite Galatians 3:5, in which the apostle proves the true doctrine that Christ is among believers because of the miracles done in their midst. They sometimes also add Matthew 11:5, in which John's disciples ask Jesus whether he is the true Christ, and Jesus replies, "The blind receive their sight, and the lame walk," implying that these wonderful works demonstrate that He is the Messiah.

We grant this is part of what the apostle means in calling the Corinthians to examine themselves for an experiential proof of Paul's apostleship among them, yet that cannot be the entire meaning because Christ is not said to dwell in us (according to the scriptural phrase) or to be in us merely by means of miraculous faith.

The consequential absurdity follows in the words "except ye be reprobates." Johannes Piscator (1546–1625) views *reprobates* here as opposite to those who are predestinated to salvation. But I prefer Theodore Beza's (1519–1605) view of this word as describing a corrupt and unsound mind. Thus the Corinthians could easily discover the work of Christ in and among themselves, unless their understanding was in part depraved. For Paul did not suggest total unsoundness in them, as is evident by his use of the Greek, which mitigates the speech and is therefore translated by some as, "Unless you are unsound in something."

A reprobate mind is a corrupt mind, according to Titus 1:16. Second Timothy 3:8 also refers to "men of corrupt minds, reprobate concerning the faith." Although we do not take reprobates here as the opposite of those predestinated to salvation, yet I do not see why we may not well translate it reprobates, not regarding them to have no hope of salvation, but instead as what the Scripture calls "reprobate silver" in Jeremiah 6:30, meaning something that has no worth or value in trade. Though the apostle is writing to the entire church at Corinth, each individual believer is called to observe the duty he asks of them. That is denied by Willem van Est (1542–1613), who avoided orthodox arguments for assurance of faith by saying that it may be more easily known that Christ is in a certain church or congregation rather than in the heart of an individual believer. For the text speaks not of Christ being in His doctrine and ordinances among them, which indeed is easily discerned, but of His spiritually inhabiting them by sanctifying grace.

From this text, then, we may make two general observations:

+ Observation 1: It is a duty of special concern for the people of God to be assured of the true and saving work of grace in themselves, for by means of this assurance they know they are not unsound hypocrites.

+ Observation 2: There are certain marks and signs of grace by which a person may discern what he is.

True Knowledge of Grace

A practical, experimental knowledge of grace far transcends a mere notional or theoretical knowledge of it. It is like the difference between someone who has heard that honey is sweet, and someone who has tasted it. A rule among the Hebrews is that words of knowledge may sometimes signify affections in the heart as well as actions in life. How good it would be if words always distinguished true Christians from false.

In former times Christians labored much for experimental knowledge, while today they are satisfied with mere brain knowledge. In medicine we contemptuously call a person an empiric if he goes by experience alone and has no knowledge of the nature of things. To be an empiric in Christianity, however, may be understood in a good sense. Bernard of Clairvaux (1090–1153) rightly said that in reading books we should not look for science as much as for the savoriness of truth upon our hearts.

But the apostle goes on to command us to prove and try ourselves by actual outworkings of grace in our lives, which enable us to persuade ourselves that we are recipients of regeneration, thereby enabling us to conclude that we are believers.[1] We prove or try ourselves by applying the notes and marks of faith of which Scripture speaks, and thereby acquire an experimental feeling of the actual exercise of them. Philippians 1:9 speaks of experimental knowledge as the inward savory sense and feeling of divine things upon the heart.

The Necessity of Assurance

The necessity of having assurance about this practical, experimental work of grace, by which we are enabled to

---

1. Burgess calls the actual outworkings of grace *actu secunda*, that is, secondary acts, that flow out of the *actu primo*, that is, the habit of grace, which is inseparable from regeneration.

discern the true from the counterfeit, is evident on several grounds:

1. Our Savior's strong emphasis on this point in His sermons. The heathen say, "When a wise man speaks, he opens the rich treasures and wardrobe of his mind." If this is true of a wise man, it is even truer of Christ, in whom are all the treasures of wisdom. Of all the practical points in theology He makes, our Savior most frequently speaks about what is evident in His first parable, recorded in Matthew 13:3. This story shows the difference between true and counterfeit grace. Luke 8:8 says that after Jesus finished telling the parable, He cried, "He that hath ears to hear, let him hear." Crying is not attributed to Christ's speech unless His affections are very earnest and the subject is of great importance. He is speaking to a multitude of people who have thronged Him and are now listening intently to His words. Yet Jesus declares that few have a good and honest heart to receive the word.

Our Savior says that in our use of the ordinances we may perceive such change in us that we think we have joy, faith, or some kind of reformation, yet we still might not be the good and right soil that truly receives the word. That is a challenge for us to stay attuned to the word until we are truly assured of our salvation.

Our Savior offers another parable to make this point. In Matthew 25:1, He speaks of ten virgins or young women who have preserved themselves from the idolatries and gross vices of the world. They all have lamps and are confidently walking to meet the bridegroom. One virgin is no different from the other until the bridegroom comes, revealing those who have not brought sufficient oil to keep their lamps burning. This parable suggests that someone with much knowledge, such as a professor, may have a false, imperfect, or counterfeit work of grace. He lives in comfort and confidence, believing that his spiritual condition is right before God. He does not find out otherwise until it is too late.

Again, in Matthew 7:24–26, Jesus speaks of two builders, one who builds upon sand and the other upon rock. This parable represents two kinds of believers. One makes a profession of faith and follows the way of Christianity. He is truly rooted in Christ, the Rock. The other seems to be a believer, but he, like the majority of Christians, does not dig deep enough. His faith, repentance, and joy are set upon shifting sand. The consequence is that his "fall thereof was great." The damnation of such people will be truly awful when all their religious duties and external professions crash to the ground. How woeful it will be when they are rent from God, despite all the duties they have trusted in for salvation. Our Savior warns in Matthew 7:22 that many will call to Him at that day, claiming they have prophesied in His name and eaten and drunk in His presence. These people offered many sacrifices and received many sacraments, but

Christ will say, "I never knew you" (v. 23). It is critical that we are not deceived about the work of saving grace within us. We must keep our eyes focused on God's true work of grace, lest we build our spiritual state with counterfeit coin.

2. The tendency to make false assumptions about our faith. The experiential knowledge of faith is of special concern because of our innate tendency to mistake true faith from false. Augustine said that error and dangerous tendencies are more easily made in expounding the doctrine of the Trinity than in other doctrines. That also applies, however, to the apostle's command to examine and prove our faith because of the deceitfulness of our hearts and our failure to distinguish between many false shapes and forms of faith. Scripture's admonitions to be searching our hearts and communing with our hearts argue the difficulty of being fully acquainted with what is in them.

Roman Catholics press this point too far, as if no one can tell if they truly love God or have a sincere heart. In due course this will be shown to be false. It is true, however, that we have so much self-love and carnal confidence in ourselves that we can easily assume that we are what we ought to be. Ask one person after another about their eternal state: who is not confident that he is regenerated, that he has a saving interest in Christ, and that his heart is good? And why is this so? Because he does not faithfully compare himself to the marks and character of true grace, and does not diligently apply them to himself. The Jews and Pharisees could not be beaten out of their vain hopes and carnal confidences that they truly kept the law of God. Therefore, the apostle uses the emphatic word of a Jew in Romans 2:17 to say, "Thou…restest in the law." The Jews and Pharisees found security in the law as if it were an admirable privilege and testimony of God's love. Christ promises "rest unto your souls" in Matthew 11:29, but no load of sin could burden the Pharisees because they believed they were already at rest.

In much the same way, some Christians rest in knowing the doctrine of the gospel and in the outward use of ordinances without ever feeling the weight of sin. It would be better for those people to pray with fear and to eat their bread with trembling and astonishment rather than to be hypocrites who are carnally and falsely persuaded of their good condition. Many so-called Christians are like glowworms or rotten white trees made of base materials, shining only on the outside! Therefore what should be fastened upon the gates of the whole world, upon every door and every post is, "Examine, prove yourselves."

3. *The danger of miscarrying in this matter.* Oh, the confusion that fell upon the foolish virgins when their lack of oil was discovered! How careful we are to avoid taking

counterfeit coin. But it is even more dangerous to mistake counterfeit repentance for true repentance, counterfeit faith for true faith. If your praying and profession of faith is not good and true, you will be forever undone.

In Hebrews 6:4, the apostle speaks of some who experienced things many of us have not attained to. They had been "enlightened," had "tasted of the heavenly gift" (the good word of God), and were "partakers of the Holy Ghost." Yet the apostle also says in Hebrews 6:9, "We are persuaded better things of you, and things that accompany salvation." What thunder and lightning accompanies this teaching, that better things than illumination, than participation in holy things, do accompany true salvation! We cry out with the disciples, "This is a hard saying; who then can be saved?"

Yet it is the truth. And as ministers of God's Word we say that unless your righteousness exceeds that of outward profession, of repeating sermons, of family duties, and of the common works of God's Spirit—all of which those who have temporary faith possess, you cannot enter the kingdom of heaven. We pray for better things of you, things that will surely accompany salvation.

4. *The difficulty of distinguishing between true and counterfeit grace.* It is difficult to distinguish between true grace and its counterfeit. It is so difficult that some divines view the work of grace in the temporary believer as different from that in the regenerated person only in

terms of degree rather than kind, though this is false. If it is so hard for theologians to set the doctrinal bounds, how much more difficult it is for ordinary Christians to mark out the right way!

A hypocrite feels joy, sorrow, and sweetness in the ordinances, and so does the godly. But to show how one is deceived and the other is not is difficult, even though they do indeed differ as much as one who dreams differs from one who is truly awake. Paul's admonition to "try and prove" supposes that a man must have knowledge of the rule and the characteristics that describe such a grace. He must also have skill in applying these notes to himself and to do this without the temptation to do otherwise, with much attention and perseverance.

In doctrinal controversies the great question is, What is the true church that does not err, and what are the essential marks that constitute a church? Similarly, in practical matters, these are the great questions: What is true grace? Do I possess true grace? What are the marks to decipher this? As for the former questions, we wish we had a visible, infallible judge to determine such a matter so there might no longer be dispute. Likewise, we desire a peculiar revelation from heaven that should by name say to us that we are among those Christians in whom is no guile.

5. *Assurance of faith has many advantages.* Manifold advantages will come to us when we have attained to

an experimental knowledge of ourselves. First, we will reckon all our former knowledge of divine things and its parts as a tinkling cymbal that is no longer admirable. Once we have the inward feeling of holy things upon our hearts, we will bewail all the duties, spiritual conversation, and religious performances formerly done by us, as if we had been a parrot with no understanding of these things. If a person reads a book or map to see various countries, he has some limited knowledge of them. But if he travels into those countries and sees their towns and buildings, he will admit that his former knowledge of them was lame compared to what he has now.

The queen of Sheba once heard rumors of Solomon's wisdom, but when she visited the king and came to have an experimental knowledge of his wisdom she was astonished and said, "All that I had heard was nothing to that which I saw." So it is in the matter of grace. If God works His savory inward experimental knowledge in you, you will be astonished to see the difference between what you were before that time and what you are now. All that you have heard, read, or preached is nothing to what you now feel.

It is fearful to note how many people have seen godliness, but only as on a map. They have never experienced it for themselves. Many people talk of their conversion or repentance as men talk of bringing forth a child, speaking of the matter without ever experiencing the throbs and pains of childbirth themselves (see Rom.

7:9). Paul traveled for a long time on the road of religious duties, but when he came to have an experimental knowledge of Christ, he died to his own righteousness in which he had previously lived; he became sensible of the damnable and dangerous estate he was in, whereas before his conversion he had great confidence of his good life and salvation. Thus it is with every man who has received experimental knowledge. He says, "Alas, I was alive once, and I thought I was somebody. I could pray, write sermons, and dispute with great understanding, but now I see that I did not know what true faith or godliness was. I argued much about it, but I knew nothing of God or His gracious works until now."

Second, a person with experimental knowledge has a heart that is like the Bible's counterpane. Scripture is the original, and his heart is the copy of it. The believer can read about the promises and threats of Scripture and say, "This is well proven; the case is closed." David in his Psalms and Paul in his epistles speak to a man's heart, feel his temptations, and anticipate his objections. As John 3:33 says, "He that hath received his testimony hath set to his seal that God is true." Scripture also speaks of God's sealing to us and our sealing to Him in a metaphor of civil contracts which were confirmed and declared good by their seals (see Jer. 32:10). Thus a true believer who receives the testimony of Scripture solemnly declares by his life and conversation that God is true. All who say they believe yet do not practice the effects of conversion set not their seal that God is true.

Third, experimental knowledge also deadens the believer's heart to merely human excellencies. The philosophers say that a vegetative and sensitive life is swallowed up in a rational one. So a Christian's natural life in great measure is swallowed up in his supernatural life. Corn and thorns come up together in a farmer's soil. But where grace is practiced, all weeds will be cut off. Heart feelings, not head notions, will exclude immoderate affections to worldly things. A man who has long tasted the wine of brain knowledge, once he comes to taste experimental knowledge, will declare that the new knowledge is best.

In Galatians 2:20 Paul denies that he lives, "but Christ liveth in" him. In Christ, all life is for delight. Until you take delight and experimental sweetness in holy things, your tongue may prattle about good things but your heart will not be in them. Love of the world is part of the former kind of knowledge, but not in the latter. Aristotle observed that dogs cannot hunt where the scent of sweet flowers is because the scent diverts their sense of smell. Likewise, we may not run after Christ in the sweetness of His ointments when we are inhibited by the smell of worldly delights and refreshments.

CHAPTER 2

Additional Advantages of Assurance

In addition to general notional knowledge, the true Christian gains the practical and experimental knowledge of grace in his heart. These advantages include the following.

Practical and Experimental Benefits

Enjoying the Sweetness of the Ordinances

The true, experiential Christian enjoys the sweetness and benefit of the ordinances unlike those who have only head knowledge and gifts. Many people in church administrations are like old Barzillai who lost his taste and hearing and thus did not care for David's feasts and music (2 Sam. 19:35). In Psalm 19:10 David says he prefers God's Word as "sweeter...than honey and the honeycomb." In Psalm 84 he admires the loveliness and beauty of God's ordinances. Sadly, a man without the experimental work of grace upon his soul can no more be affected with these than a blind man can appreciate color. Song of Songs 1:3 says, "Because of the savour of thy good ointments thy name is as ointment poured forth, therefore do the virgins love thee." Christ in His ordinances, like Mary breaking open a box of ointment, diffuses spiritual sweetness in church assemblies to the godly. Only the experimental Christian senses this.

Chrysostom at times preached about the hidden and choice principles of the Christian religion by saying, "Those who are initiated or admitted into the mysteries of faith know what I mean." Likewise, the minister of God who preaches about the bitterness of sin and the sadness of spiritual desertions as well as the fullness of Christ and the sweetness of experiencing His fellowship and communion, may say, "The practiced, exercised Christian knows what I mean." Formal Christians are strangers to the virtue and efficacy that are communicated in the spiritual ordinances.

In Song of Songs 4:12, the church is compared to "a garden inclosed…a spring shut up, a fountain sealed," which is to be understood not only in terms of the defense and protection God provides His church so that no one can destroy her, but also that strangers and wicked men are prevented from tasting her delicacies or smelling her sweetness. A spiritual sermon is a "fountain sealed," and the spiritual administration of a sacrament is a "garden inclosed." Formal, notional Christians do not understand or perceive the full sweetness of this. While many people crowded around our Savior, only a sick woman felt the efficacy of His healing. Likewise, many participate in the ordinances and frequent the assemblies of the church, but only a few sense the inward power of Christ in their souls.

The disciple Thomas, though upon an ill ground, said he would not believe Christ had risen unless he saw His wounds, and put his fingers into them. Likewise, do not believe your estate is good and sound unless you see and feel the efficacy of Christ in His ordinances upon you. Augustine speaks of the fatness and sweetness he experienced in God's ordinances, saying in his *Confessions*, "Sometimes Thou dost introduce me to a most rare and inward feeling, an inexplicable sweetness. If this were to come to perfection in me, I do not know to what point life might not then arrive" (X.65).

Ceasing from Needless and Vain Disputations and Looking More into the Heart

By this practical knowledge and exercise, you will be weaned from needless and vain disputations in matters of religion and will be more attentive to your own heart. In former times, the people of God were so busy looking for the touchstone and trial of grace in themselves that they did not launch out into deep and unprofitable questions. But of late, believers have become so busy in disputes and controversies and new opinions that they are neglecting this practical knowledge of grace. Such people would sooner dispute about faith than live by faith, or talk more about heavenly-mindedness than being heavenly-minded.

The result is that these trees in God's garden sprout suckers and barren boughs and bear little fruit (1 Tim. 6:4). The apostle excellently describes such a temperament as "doting about questions," which results, as is stated in the Greek, in "sickness and languishing." Just as much fretting and vexation consumes the flesh of the body, so the proud and vain affectations of new opinions pine away the soul. What is this but to think that "a stone may become bread and a serpent a fish"? The minister's duty is only to preach those things that are profitable. Thus, Jesus says, "The sower went out to sow good seed," not poisonous tares or empty chaff. Likewise, it is the private Christian's duty only to think about and study those things that will edify and build up their souls.

I would not discourage the efforts of Christians to grow in knowledge. The apostle reproves some for being babes and says that he cannot speak unto them as spiritual but carnal. Only they must know that faith includes efficacious purifying acts as well as acts of knowledge, and therefore their increase must be equal in accord with their knowledge and its efficacy. A Christian may grow in accord with the extent of his knowledge or its effectiveness. He may know more of various matters and understand them more clearly, evidently, and firmly than he did before. Though he does not know more things than he did before, yet he understands them more practically. They have a greater influence upon his heart and affections. They move and inflame him more than ever before. Even if the former way of increasing knowledge is necessary and pleasing to God, this experiential understanding is even better. So take heed that you are not like Pharaoh's lean cattle that devour many questions but are still as starved and ill-favored as ever.

When a person came with curiosity to the Savior asking the question whether there are "few that be saved," our Savior answered him, "Strive to enter in at the strait gate: for many, I say unto you, will seek to enter in, and shall not be able" (Luke 13:23, 24). This shows us the necessity of persistently pressing and urging practical knowledge upon people when they prefer to argue rather than find life. As little boys in sport compete over who can strike the most sparks with their iron, though not intending to use those sparks for something useful like kindling a fire, so many Christians strive for the most subtle and finest spun notions without ever intending to use them for the profit of their souls.

Attaining the Purpose of Knowledge, Which Is Action
By practical experience a Christian attains to the goal of all knowledge, which is to live out his Christianity. If you know these things, blessed are you if you do them. Some people have money only to tell others about it; they make no good use of it. That is as vain as having the knowledge of religion only to know, rather than to have what Titus 1:1 calls "the acknowledging of the truth which is after godliness," indicating that those who

have not the practical power of knowledge are denied to have any knowledge at all. Consequently, wicked men are often called fools because they fail to know God. A private Christian may know more of God than a learned doctor who has nothing but orthodoxy. A learned man may write and preach admirably about justifying faith, conversion, or other spiritual matters, yet this knowledge cannot be compared to what a private man or woman feels in the power of these things upon their hearts.

Some argue whether divinity is speculative or practical. This dispute can be resolved by stating upon good grounds that divinity is practical, for religion is nothing if it does not result in improving one's practice. Orthodoxy and true doctrine may be defended by books, disputations, and sermons, but above all else we must make sure that our life reflects our Christian profession. When Christ looked at a fig tree that only had leaves, He cursed it for not bearing fruit. He who knows how to do good and fails to do it commits a greater sin than one who does not know what is good. Bernard of Clairvaux said that it is very dangerous to eat meat without digesting it. True doctrine and godly living go together. In the Scriptures, Abraham's servant gave Rebekah both earrings and bracelets. Cyril applies this to Christ, who vouchsafes to His church both true faith that comes by hearing and a godly life that practices this faith through the work of her hands.

Being Settled in the Truth Leads to Endurance under Persecution

By this experimental knowledge, a man will be settled in the truth and willing to endure all persecution rather than forsake it. He will not believe fallacies or sophisms. He will not be frightened out of believing the truth, for he has tasted God and His Word, and the rule is that there is no disputing against taste. The senses of taste and feeling differ from the other senses, for they are joined to the objects themselves. The senses of seeing and hearing receive only what is intended and therefore cannot make as real and powerful an impression as tasting or feeling. Paul's experimental "knowing whom he did believe" made him bold to speak, whereas men who have a monthly or yearly faith will change their opinions as often as their garments because they have not felt the power of truth upon their soul.

Scholastic teachers often speak of a gift of the Holy Ghost called *sapience*, by which they mean that there can be a certain light about divine things whereby some may see and taste by experience or, as others say, may contemplate God with a certain experimental sweetness in the affections. Despite this view, the apostle in Hebrews 5:14 would have them by reason of use have their senses exercised to discern both good and evil. The apostle attributes to the mind what is properly speaking the organs of sense to the body, but he also applies them to the soul because of the intuitive and experimental knowledge the soul ought to have in good things. Therefore, he speaks of the use and custom of the people of God in spiritual discerning.

It is no wonder, then, that Hebrews 11:1 declares faith to be the real substance of things believed in the soul. Faith is an undeniable conviction of the mind because when grace operates upon the soul, it makes a true impression. The whole work and way of grace is compared to life in Galatians 2 because it is real, not a figment of imagination or fancy. Thus Hebrews 13:9 tells us, "Be not carried about with divers and strange doctrines. For it is a good thing that the heart be established with grace."

The apostle says that grace and godliness establish and settle the heart. By contrast, men who are led aside into errors are like chaff, which, because of its emptiness and lightness, is blown this way and that. Thus a man who is empty of grace and not consolidated by the power of it upon his heart will run from one opinion to another. A savory inward knowledge of divine truth is excellent ballast in the soul. It keeps the heart firm in the truth. It unites the heart to holy things which are the best and the sweetest, and preserves it from hypocrisy, double-mindedness, and inconstancy.

A man's heart may be inclined toward good things at one time and the things of the world at other times, resulting in a heart that is divided between the Creator and the creature. Such a heart lacks real and experimental knowledge of the goodness of God. Christ says, "He that drinketh of this water shall never thirst again," that is, shall experience an utter lack of thirst. Now how great a mercy it is to be kept from double-mindedness, which the apostle describes as a wave that is sometimes tossed up high to the heavens then sinks down into the sea, or like grasshoppers that leap up toward heaven but immediately fall back to the ground. When the temptations of profit and pleasure come, they are easily repulsed by a heart that feels better things. Until you have an inward feeling and joy about the things of God, you will not be able to withstand other temptations, but you will always be striving to make possible that which our Savior has pronounced impossible: to serve God and mammon.

Impediments to Finding Proof of Experimental Knowledge in Ourselves

The duty of examining and proving ourselves is like the compound that the high priest made of choice materials. It is difficult to find proof of experimental knowledge because of the following impediments.

Self-Love, Carnal Confidence, and the Temptation to Unbelief

One danger of proving and examining ourselves is that we are possessed with self-love and carnal confidence, and upon this foundation it is impossible to build a good superstructure. All of the piercing and discovering sermons that the prophets and Christ delivered to the Jews and Pharisees could not shake their rotten foundation because of their carnal confidence and vain trust in themselves.

Therefore, when you set upon the duty of examining yourself, you must say, "Lord, I come not in any love of myself. I can as easily judge and condemn myself as a hypocrite (if such I shall be found) as to be approved as an upright one. O Lord, it shall not seem a hard thing to me, if I perceive that I have labored in vain for these many years. O Lord, it shall be far from a matter of discontentment—indeed, I shall rejoice—if I shall be put into a sound and right way of holiness."

But how many search the grounds, principles, and ends of their actions with as much negligence as officers who go to alehouses and unlawful meetings? They are unwilling to see their hidden works of darkness. Proverbs 28:26 says, "He that trusteth in his own heart is a fool." It is desperate folly to believe that your heart will deal truly with you. Hence the prophet Jeremiah says that our hearts are "desperately wicked," or crafty, and will beguile and deceive us without much caution. So the duty of self-examination is ridiculous and mere mockery unless we resolve to become impartial judges. It is like disputing with the Roman Catholic Church, which says the true church cannot err, and then says that she is the true church. She is thus incurable and without hope of healing. Proverbs 16:2 says, "All the ways of a man are clean in his own eyes; but the LORD weigheth the spirits."

Trusting our hearts is one way to blind us, but another extreme is giving way to the temptation of unbelief. This is when a godly soul sets itself against itself and takes everything that he does as hypocritical. With this mindset, he will draw false conclusions in self-examination. As the carnal man fails to see his sins, so the tempted Christian sees only his sins. The one believes everything is done with a good heart, while the other claims no good is possible. As a man who would see his face in the water makes no commotion or trouble at all, so he who would rightly judge his heart must take heed of carnal confidence on one side, and unbelief on the other.

An Erroneous Principle

A second dangerous principle is concluding that an action may be declared good if the end result appears good, regardless of the principles, ends, or motives for the action. This principle destroys many thousands of people. Jehu did what he thought was God's will, so he boasted that he was zealous for God. "Come see my zeal," he said. But though his actions were great and of high value for the church of God, yet God would avenge Himself because of them. Who would think God would be avenged on Jehu for dispossessing Jeroboam, killing Baal's priests, and starting a great reformation (Hos. 1:4)? The answer is that Jehu did not do these things with an upright heart, so God threatened him.

The Pharisees showed external righteousness, but a great gulf lay between them and true godliness. Jesus called them vipers who looked glorious but were full of poison. They looked so holy, yet like the serpent they ate the dust of the earth and fed upon earthly advantages. A man therefore must have the eyes of an eagle or be like one of Ezekiel's living creatures that was full of eyes so that he may see to the bottom of his ways. Your profession, your family duties, and your religious performances are plainly visible to others. Everyone may read these acts, yet your ends and motives are as secret as the foundations and roots of things that lie underground.

The first letters of a book may be garnished with so many flourishes that we can hardly tell what they say. Paul distinguished between a Jew outwardly and inwardly by noting that circumcision of the flesh was not the same as circumcision of the heart. This difference is especially true of the ends and motives that distinguish moral actions from immoral ones. Two may be in a family. Both pray and both mourn for their sin, yet one does this out of a pure motive from God and to God and therefore is right. The other does this with the wrong motive and for self, not God. He is thus rejected by God. Who is sufficient for so great a duty as self-examination!

Judging Ourselves by False Weights

The duty of examining and proving ourselves supposes there is a sure standard to use so we are not deceived.

That rule is the Word of God. But in matters of doctrine some men have left the Scriptures as the sure rule and taken up antiquity, universality, tradition, and the like as their guide. By these means they have fallen into the ditch. In matters of godliness we should try ourselves according to the characters and signs that Scripture gives. We should put aside principles of the world, the applause of others, and the conversation of others, for we are all like men put in a hospital, where everyone is either wounded or lame or is in some way diseased, and, therefore, none is offensive to the other.

Mistaking the Object of Our Inquiry

We may mistake what godliness is and think it is in us when it is not. People err seriously when they mistake a good nature, morality, civility, or common graces of God's Spirit for godliness, so that when they see these they conclude all is well. This is like a man who mistakes lead or copper for gold and thinks himself rich because he has them. Those who would not be deceived in this matter must consider what Scripture says about the nature and properties of godliness, concluding that godliness is no less than or inferior to what Scripture says. If a man does not reach for directions from Scripture, he will be like a glowworm that thinks he is the sun. We will enlarge later on these things.

Concluding Applications

Let us therefore set about this work with all diligence, fear, and trembling. How much better it is to eat and drink, and to pray and hear with fear and trembling of heart than to be falsely secure in our spiritual condition. Do not believe your own hearts in times of danger, or fears of death, or any sudden fits. Consider how Pharaoh and Ahab cried out because of their sin under the judgments of God, but were falsely motivated.

Seek pure motivations. In civil law, no credit is given to testimony obtained by the use of a rack because torture and pain will make a man say anything to ease his suffering. In times of trouble and fear, even a false heart will admit wrong to get relief. In this life we may satisfy ourselves and others with a verbal profession and external diligence in holy duties. Yet on the judgment day, we will be astonished by what God has to say to us and will be silent before Him. In the parable given by Jesus, a man came to a feast without a wedding garment. When asked why he was not properly attired, the man was speechless. He did not plead poverty or difficulty in getting a wedding garment, but was struck speechless, as if he had a muzzle placed over his mouth. In the judgment day all the crookedness, subtleties, and false pretexts of your own heart will be revealed, and you will be forced to see and acknowledge the truth.

CHAPTER 3

Can Hypocrites Attain Practical Knowledge about Religion?

Let us now address some practical questions about those who claim to be Christians but are not. May these hypocrites attain some measure of practical knowledge in matters of religion? Does the fire, which is warm and filled with light in the godly, become filled also with light in hypocrites? Can unregenerate men go no farther than mere knowledge and illumination? May not this oil poured upon their heads also fall down upon their wills and affections? Since they have imperfect knowledge, may they also have imperfect affections about good things? If they do, how are we to discern the difference or exact limits between practical knowledge in the true believer and the hypocrite?

To consider this matter, we begin by saying that in general there are three kinds of people who claim to be Christians, and thus think to be partakers in all the rights and privileges of the covenant of grace. Let us examine each of these so-called Christians.

Types of So-Called Christians

Scandalous Christians

The first so-called Christians claim the name and outward ordinances of Christianity but have not the least influence or power from it, for "in works they deny him" (Titus 1:16). These people are like prescription boxes which have been labeled as a helpful drug but in fact contain deadly poison. These so-called Christians are heathen in their actions. The prophets spoke out against the kings of Israel and Judah who did evil in the sight of God, saying they were like the princes of Sodom and Gomorrah who were circumcised in the flesh yet continued to do evil. They are hypocrites; they are Christians *without* Christ, or even *against* Christ.

In some respects, however, these so-called Christians may be better than the heathen. An early Christian apologist, Arnobius (d. 330), said somewhat crudely that a Christian even in fornication is better than a most chaste idolater. Yet in other respects this kind of Christian is far worse, for he has no real and saving benefit from Christ. He is a dead corpse that is covered by sweet fragrant flowers, but not in the least degree made less odious by them. Indeed, it is an aggravation of the wickedness of such people when they use moral philosophy and the principles of reason to cure their outward ungodliness while remaining inwardly unchanged. The truths of Christianity, which have the power to regenerate the heart and give birth to a new nature, do far more than change the skin of men. Yet the majority of those who are baptized into the name of Christ have the Christian name, but nothing else. They do not derive their power from Christ but are like a dead hand or withered branch whose whole lives are a continual blasphemy against the gospel of Christ.

Historical and Temporary Believers

Another kind of Christian shows some influence of the operations of the Spirit of God, yet is like an embryo that proves abortive (see the second and third kinds of hearers in Matthew 13). The first of these receive the Word of God but then fail to develop roots and grow. They have the kind of historical faith that the devils possess. It is no real faith at all, but, at most, only a human assent.

The latter group are usually said by theologians to have temporary faith. This kind of faith differs from historical faith because, like true faith, it includes some affections both in the person revealing it, who is God, and in the content being revealed. Thus, temporary faith sees who God is in the content revealed, whereas historical faith has no affections at all.

Temporary believers are in fact carnal and unregenerate, differing from true believers as much as copper differs from dung. In comparison to the godly they are counterfeit and false, though in comparison to profane men they may be like pearls and stars. They have some practical experience of divine truths upon them; however, the Spirit of Christ does not dwell in them because they are not members of the body of Christ. The soul of a man cannot control a limb that is separated from the body. Neither does the Spirit of Christ operate savingly but in the body of Christ. Nevertheless, the Spirit of God works as an outward efficient cause in breathing upon the temporary believers. The Spirit does not work savingly in them, but only uses them as an instrument for the good of the church. There is great variance in this type of Christian. Some temporary believers have a greater measure of these workings than others, just as temporary believers go beyond historical believers.

True Believers

These Christians are incorporated into Christ's body and so receive a vivifying influence from Him as a living branch in the vine or a living member in the body. They are animated by the Spirit, though with an infinite disproportion compared to what is in Christ, their head. They are born of God, have an immortal seed in them, and will never perish because Christ will not lose any living, mystical members of His body. These Christians alone have a proper, clear, and rich experiential knowledge of Christ's sufferings and resurrection upon their soul. They differ from other so-called Christians, not gradually (as some think), but specifically. A regenerate man, though the lowest of that company, is as far removed from the unregenerate as the heavens are from the sublunary bodies, for the works of God's Spirit upon hypocrites, even if increased ever so high, do not rise up to saving grace, just as copper will never be gold.

In the next place, observe that while hypocrites or temporary believers do not attain to what is saving, yet the works of God's Spirit are great upon them, and many experimental motions of the truths of Christianity are wrought upon them. Let us look at some of these to awaken you and make you tremble, lest you might not be found above them; or worse, be found not even to rise up to their level.

The Experimental Knowledge of Hypocrites
Hypocrites may attain practical experiential knowledge of the following.

The Common Gifts of the Spirit
So-called Christians may feel assistance from God. Matthew 7:22 says, "Many will say to me in that day, Lord, Lord, have we not prophesied in thy name, and in thy name have cast out devils, and in thy name done many wonderful works?" Hypocrites did these works by the power of Christ and by virtue of Him. Though we have already told you that the goal of the apostle was to prove that Christ was in them by virtue of the miracles and wonderful works they did, yet this was only a part. Saul had another spirit, not in the way of sanctification

but in political administration, whereby he had an experimental knowledge of God's power and assistance in his own calling. Likewise many Christians may sense God's assistance in duties, gifts, and abilities. They may feel the power of the Lord going along with them. Yet this has nothing to do with sanctification.

It is fearful to realize that the practical experience of God's help is the most that such people will experience. If that is not so, why do people abound in opinions and disputations, yet have little to say about mortification and vivification? They sprout suckers and leaves but do not bear fruit. The Corinthians reveal that men are more prone to desire the gifts of God's Spirit for public administration than for personal sanctification. They said that to be a good preacher, one has to be a good disputant who offers lengthy prayers, and they argue that the Spirit of God must only breathe on you but not dwell in you. They taught that God does not bestow gifts on you for any love of your soul but because of His church. Nurses who care for a prince's children will feed on delicate fare, not for their own sake but for the children's sake to whom they give milk. They are like those who preach the gospel of Christ to others but do not partake of it themselves. They are like the signs on highways that give directions to various places, but never move from the place they are at. Oh, that the ministers of God would become more like sons of thunder in this matter! You may have experienced God's enabling, enlarging, and other common gifts of His Spirit, but have you felt God renewing, sanctifying, and healing you of your lusts?

The Bitterness of Sin

Hypocrites may have some practical experience of the bitterness of sin and the terrors that result from it. We may not think that the terrors which came upon Cain and Judas were merely the result of the natural light of conscience, for such could be quickly extinguished. No, those terrors were the result of the Spirit of God convincing them of sin in their consciences. Romans 8:15 refers to the Spirit of God as the "spirit of bondage again to fear" because the Spirit works fear and trouble in the heart of a sinner, not convicting them of the sinfulness of sin, but moving them to feel the troublesome motions and stirrings of their sins in their souls. We may not say that Ahab and the Israelites cried out to God over their sins by the mere power of their natural freewill. No, they were moved by the common work of the Spirit of God. Also, there are many whose pains and wounds of heart are inflicted upon them by the preaching of the Word. When the memory of their sins is like wormwood and gall to them, this flows from the Spirit of God.

Whatever is wrought instrumentally by the Word is wrought efficiently by God's Spirit. This confirms that many men, who yet are not made new creatures, have experienced a foretaste of hell at times in their hearts.

Their consciences tell them it is a bitter thing to sin against God. And because they have experienced such wounds and blows in the past, they wrongly conclude that they have been newly born. Though their conviction has brought forth nothing but wind in all their pain, yet they rejoice as if a man-child or new creature has been born!

We may thus conclude that even one who is a wild olive and not yet implanted in Christ may have the inward feeling of God's displeasure for sin. They may even be able to tell you of a time when they could not eat or drink or sleep but cried out, "Oh, my sins, my sins, my sins!" yet they do not demonstrate Christ dwelling in them.

Desires and Affections for Things That Are Good

Those who are not true Christians may have some apprehension of the goodness of spiritual things. They may also have some general affections and desires for them. In such a condition they cry out as the people did in John 6:34: "Lord, evermore give us this bread." Christ told people He was the Manna and Bread of Life. He also spoke of the benefits that come to those who feast on Him, for He, unlike temporary bread, not only nourishes but gives life. Thus those who truly listened to Jesus responded, in a confused manner but with some good intentions, "Give us evermore this bread." They were like Peter during the transfiguration of Christ, who asked to stay upon the mountain, not knowing what that meant. Balaam also asked for something he did not understand. When viewing the happiness of the people of God he was so moved that he said he wished to die the death of the righteous. Others, too, may be so affected by the spiritual ordinances and worship of God that they declare, "How beautiful are thy tabernacles, O Israel!" Yet often such people are deluded because they have had brief seasons of good affections and desires, while the overwhelming bent of their souls is toward evil.

Sweetness and Joy in the Ordinances

Some hypocrites have experienced sweetness and joy in God's ordinances and some assurances of God's favor flowing out of this. As Matthew 13:20 says, they received the word "with joy." John's hearers were said for a while to rejoice in his light. Ezekiel's prophecies were received by listeners "as a pleasant song." Those without the things that accompany salvation have "tasted the good word of God, and the powers of the world to come" (Heb. 6:5). They have tasted God's Word as Jonathan tasted a little honey, but they did not eat of its fullness. The true people of God ate Christ's flesh and drank His blood till rivers of living water flowed out of their belly. From these experimental tastings arose some assurance of their spiritual welfare. The foolish virgins with boldness and no suspicion of their lack of oil went forth to meet their bridegroom. Yet when he came, many of them were found without enough oil to keep their lamps lit. Now this is a matter of great importance, for people whose hearts have been at any time sweetened and mollified in the ordinances of God may falsely assume that they have eaten the bread of life.

A Changed Life

Hypocrites may experience such an experimental working that their lives and conversations show some degree of alteration and change. But the change is only temporary. As 2 Peter 2 teaches, these apostates, who returned to their own vomit, never had true grace. Yet they are said to have once escaped the pollutions of the world through the knowledge of Christ. Therefore they are called virgins, though they are foolish ones, as they were only kept from the profaneness of others.

We might think that people who have experienced all this would have to be partakers of true grace. This is not the case. Those who stole may steal no more, those who were drunk may drink no more, those who were filthy may now be clean; but yet as swine are swine by nature, they may be washed of their mire yet remain unregenerate and filthy still. By these instances you see that even men who are not in the faith after a sanctifying and saving manner may yet have many apparent works of grace on their soul.

The Differences between True Christians and False

There are many differences between true Christians and hypocrites. I will discuss them only briefly here, as we will consider them in more detail later.

Differences in Nature

That which is in the godly differs from that which is in the most refined hypocrite, as much as gold differs from dross or true pearls differ from counterfeit. Hence the fourth ground or kind of hearer in Matthew 13 is only said to have a good and honest heart. The soil of one ground or kind of hearer differs essentially from the other. This becomes abundantly clear in that the promises of justification and eternal life are not made to any kind of faith that a hypocrite possesses, but they are made only to the faith of a godly man, even though he has only a small degree of saving faith. Thus, an infant in true grace may receive Christ by the hand of faith, while a giant-like hypocrite cannot do so.

Differences in Clearness and Evidence

What hypocrites know about the things of God is confused. It is like a flash of sudden lightning rather than a permanent and abiding light. A little sip or taste of heavenly things cannot enable a man to fully comprehend the excellence and worth of them. Therefore hypocrites see these things as people who are not perfectly cured of blindness, who see "men as trees, walking" (Mark 8:24). It is true that even the holiest see only in part. David prayed that his eyes would be opened to see the wonderful things in God's law. Paul also prayed for the Ephesians "that the God of our Lord Jesus Christ, the Father of glory, may give unto you the spirit of wisdom and revelation in the knowledge of him" (Eph. 1:17). Yet this is not like the blindness of the hypocrite, who guesses at what is right rather than exercising proper judgment in godly things.

Differences in Operation

The experience of the godly inclines them spiritually, makes them more holy, and carries them out of themselves, whereas all that an unsound Christian does ends in carnal effects, and makes him puffed up, vainly confident in himself. Thus the Pharisees, who abounded in the duties of the law, also gave way to great corruptions that contradicted the law. A Pharisee praying or a Pharisee giving alms was a Pharisee in all the power of his corruption. John 3:6 says, "That which is born of the flesh is flesh; and that which is born of the Spirit is spirit." This flesh extends not only to a person's sins and corruptions but also to his duties. Therefore, the duties of a person must be spiritual in nature as well as in effect. They must leave him more humble, more dependent upon Christ and His grace, more mortified to the world and its temptations. A man's religious duties may be the stage upon which all his lusts act. He may be like the Pharisees who did all things "to be seen of men" (Matt. 23:5).

Application

In conclusion, let us not be quick to think we are good and right, for woeful indeed are the deceptions and schemes of the heart. What may you not be and do and yet still be unsound? Oh, how burdensome will it be when men shall say, "Lord, have we not been engaged in Thy service? Lord, have we not mourned in Thy presence? Have we not rejoiced in the good Word that has been preached to us?" Yet God may reject this, saying we did not act upon sound and sincere grounds and therefore did not do it for Him. He may yet say, "Depart from me, all ye workers of iniquity" (Luke 13:27).

Put aside all thoughts, disputes, and meditations on other things and mind this one necessary thing. You may dispute about what a true church, a true ministry, and true ordinances may be, but oh, consider whether there is true grace in your heart. The Pharisees kept the feasts of purification and cleansed the temple, but they were foul and unclean in their souls. God declared His invisible attributes of wisdom, power, and goodness in the visible works He did in the creation of the world. So we too must manifest that secret and hidden efficacy of Christ in us by a powerful and vigorous life of godliness. Such a life is a miracle that will confirm that you are of God.

When pride tickles you and would puff you up, say as Augustine did, "When you think you are a sheep, perhaps God knows you are a goat, and when despair and unbelief assault you, say that you think you are a goat, and then perhaps God knows you are a sheep." Of course, we do not mean to persuade true Christians to doubt or to commend uncertainty as Roman Catholics do. However, as the apostle Peter says, in holy fear and trembling, we must make our calling and election sure (2 Peter 1:10).

CHAPTER 4

Assurance May Be Experienced

We come to the second doctrine, which, though only implied, yet is of necessary use. The apostle who is pressing readers to try whether they are in Christ and in faith or not does thereby suppose that there are such signs and symptoms of this state and condition that a man diligently attending thereunto by the help of God's Spirit may come to be assured that he is in such a state, despite the arguments of the Flemish Jesuit priest, Martin Becanus (1563–1624).

It is argued that the Corinthians must have lacked assurance about their spiritual state because it would have been pointless and absurd for the apostle to exhort them to examine themselves if they had possessed assurance. The answer to this argument is easy. Although the Corinthians might de facto not have assurance, yet the apostle's urging this upon them supposes that assurance is possible. What is more, he says it is their duty to have it, although it is also true that no one in this life holds such certainty as the saints in heaven have, which excludes all weaknesses. Therefore the certainty for which God's people reach has its degrees and changes.

Scripture clearly describes the characters and signs of the state of grace such that a godly man, by the faithful application of them to himself under the guidance and enabling of the Spirit of God, may be assured that he is in such a state.

Our examination of this doctrine includes three main parts:

1. Assurance and certainty
2. The signs and marks of grace
3. The work of God's Spirit in assurance

Much excellent practical matter will flow from each of these fountains, so marvel not if I seem to be lengthy on this subject, for it is a subject of the greatest concern. If men are willing to spend so much time and cost in evidencing their titles and proprieties in land or earthly goods, how much more diligent should they be about heavenly matters!

Assurance and Certainty

In speaking about the matter of assurance or certainty, let us take note of the following twelve propositions about assurance.

1. *Assurance may be had in various ways.* There is a certainty of sense, such as what Thomas asked for by

putting his fingers into Christ's wounds. The philosophers say this kind of certainty is infallible about its proper object if there is no defect or impediment in the faculty of sense.

There is also a certainty of science and knowledge, which is either of first principles agreed upon by all without any discourse or debate or else of such conclusions as are deduced from those principles.

Lastly, there is a certainty that arises from the authority of those who witness or declare such things. The testimony of someone whom I believe to be the supreme truth, and infallible about such things, begets a firm and sure persuasion that they are true. This authority is twofold. It may be *human*, which involves men whose witness is more or less worthy of credit depending on their quality or number, resulting in more or less certainty from that witness. But this witness breeds only human faith or moral certainty. It is to be feared that the greatest number of Protestants even in matters of religion have no more than this human faith in believing what is based upon no higher a motive than human tradition or the authority of man.

This authority may also be *divine*. This is God's authority and revelation, which begets an undoubted assent that cannot be conquered by any contrary temptation. This certainty of faith is above certainty of sense or reason because the ground of it is firm and immutable. Though the nature of things believed is far above our understanding (as in the doctrine of the Trinity and the incarnation of Christ), the testimony of them is so clear and evident that the certainty of faith may not be called obscure, as the Roman Catholics say. Thomas Aquinas is right in saying that no one believes that which he does not view as credible, and therefore in everything believed there is a clear evidence of the grounds why it is believed though there is not always clarity about the thing assented to.

You may ask what kind of certainty the people of God have about their being in the state of grace in Christ. I say it is partly a certainty of faith and partly of sense that is spiritual and wrought by the Spirit of God in us and far transcends probable conjectures and moral persuasions arising in us because of the bodily affections or dispositions of joy and grief that we sometimes find in ourselves, which are also found in hypocrites who at many times seem to be partakers of such emotions.

2. *A man may be assured he is wicked.* A person may be assured that the condition he lives in is damnable. He may be assured that he is without the state of grace as long as he continues in his state of wickedness. So we may truly say to many who read this book: "Examine yourselves, try yourselves, whether you be in the flesh and power of sin or not; know ye not that the devil dwelleth and reigneth in you?" The apostle asks this type of question in 2 Corinthians 13:5. He says

in Galatians 5:19 that the works of the flesh are manifest; therefore, those who continually practice gross sins ought to conclude that they are in the state of gall and wormwood and thus have no portion in Christ and His benefits. Oh, that such sinners would make practical judgments against themselves, for this might be effectual preparation to awaken and rouse them out of their false sense of security. Instead, through self-flattery and a groundless persuasion of God's mercy, they utterly destroy themselves.

Although a man may for the present conclude that he is in a state of sin and death, he may not assure himself that he is reprobated by God and that he has such signs upon him that he can never be saved. No man can come to such a certainty through Scripture. If God does not assure believers by an extraordinary way of particular revelation, much less may we think He will assure the reprobate of damnation that way. We therefore speak of the *present* state of a wicked man. Let each person examine his soul and come to a peremptory conclusion about how matters are between God and his soul. He must not live in vain hope, knowing not what to do or what will become of him. How many are there who on their deathbed cry out, "Live I cannot and die I dare not, though I must!" Do you still not see the indications of plague upon your soul? Are not your oaths, your lusts, your neglect of holy duties a full demonstration that your heart is barren of all grace?

3. It is easier for a particular church to know it is a true visible church than for a Christian to know he is a true believer. For a church to know it is a true visible church, it must only have the notes and marks that are external, such as the pure preaching of the Word with an external receiving of it or submission to it. A man may conclude this church is a true church if it bears these marks. But the truth of grace in a man's heart requires the internal and secret operation of God's Spirit by a powerful and most effectual change of a man's soul.

Now in looking for the notes and marks of a true church, some take general marks that are common to false churches, such as the Roman Catholic signs of universality, antiquity, and temporal felicity. Others may consider useless and of no profit the whole dispute about the marks of a church, such as the Remonstrant theologian Simon Episcopius (1583–1643). Others choose marks that are far too broad, which any hypocrite may attain to, such as baptism, morality, and external conformity to God's law. Others, such as the antinomians, completely overthrow the doctrine of assurance by the signs of grace and say it is altogether useless to preach about them. Later we will refute this argument.

The Roman Catholic theologian Willem van Est would say that the apostle's exhortation in our text is only useful for trial, to determine whether a church is a true church and whether Christ dwells in her by true doctrine, miracles, and ordinances. But that cannot be the total meaning of this text, partly, because every believer did not experience Christ's indwelling by miracles and therefore could not have acknowledged Paul's ministerial power. Paul would not have taught that, considering what 2 Corinthians 13:5 and Ephesians 3:17 have to say about love and faith. So when Christ is said to dwell in our hearts by faith, this refers to justifying faith. Certainly Christ is in us as we are in Christ, for when Job 14 and many other texts are put together, we see that we are not in Christ by faith of miracles and that therefore He is not in us by such a faith.

4. No man can by a natural light or evidence in him be assured of the grace wrought in his soul. It is God's Spirit who seals to us what we are. Just as a man cannot see the sun except by the light of the sun, neither can he see Christ or His graces in himself but by the Spirit of Christ. Hence a man may be in a state of grace and not know it, like a child in the womb who is heir to a great inheritance but does not yet understand it.

It is not in the power of a man's free will to subdue and conquer sin, for that is the work of the Spirit of God in sanctification. Likewise, the light of our natural understanding cannot assure us of the things of God in us, for that belongs to the Spirit of adoption in us. Hence a man by nature is destitute of all comfort and grace. His heart is like a hell in which the unquenchable fire of lust never goes out. In it there are worms of doubts and fears that perpetually gnaw at him and never die. Because the promises of assurance are divine and supernatural, we have no more inclination to have them by nature than we do to obey the commands of God, which requires holiness. Just as a man who is unconverted resists the Spirit of God in conviction and sanctification, so too may a converted and humbled man resist the Spirit's loving ministry of comforting and witnessing to him.

Hence the people of God are engaged in spiritual combat and conflict between corruption and holiness as well as between doubt and faith. Assurance therefore does not necessarily follow the work of grace in us as heat follows the light of the fire, but is separable from it. As we see in many of David's psalms, the shepherd who was full of grace and holiness yet was often in darkness and failed to feel God's presence with him, or His love for him. This should make us keep with all fear and trembling any measure of assurance that we possess, knowing that if we sin it away, it may be as difficult to call it back into our souls again as bidding the sun to stand still in the heavens.

5. *There are four special privileges and mercies about which a Christian may be assured.* Even in this life, a Christian may be assured of his election, remission of sin, sanctification, and perseverance until future glory. The assurance of our sanctification must be the foundation for the other certainties. We may have no certainty

of predestination, justification, or glorification if we are not certain of renovation in us. We ought therefore to diligently attend to this, for someone who has a false persuasion about God's grace in him is also falsely persuaded of his pardon from sin and of his salvation, and finally all his hopes will fail him. Therefore if you would have the confidence that your sins are forgiven and such boldness as to hope for salvation, what works or fruit is there of sanctifying grace in you? You must begin there, for if this foundation is not laid, you will build in vain. Not that we are to trust in our graces but we should gather God's love in these graces as signs and testimonies, for, as Bernard said, our certainty rests on the merit of God, not on our merit. According to Ambrose, we should say, "I will not glory because I am just, but I will glory because I have been redeemed. I will not glory because I am exempt from sins, but I will glory because my sins have been forgiven."

6. *It is a sad delusion for an ungodly man to be persuaded that his state is good when it is nothing but sin and death.* We pity those who are bewitched or possessed with devils, but the most terrible possession is when a man is deluded by the devil appearing as an angel of light. Thus the Pharisees blasphemed when they accused Christ of having a demon when they themselves were possessed by one.

You who justify yourselves are all prone to this kind of wrong judgment. Every man's ways appear right in his own eyes, but the Lord ponders the heart. In this bewitchery most men live, even such as those in the church at Laodicea, who were persuaded of their riches and fullness when indeed they were naked and empty. They needed the spiritual eye salve that would open their eyes to rightly judge themselves.

Likewise, how great your confusion will be when your gold is found dross; your wine, water; your graces, corruption; and your goodness, nothing but sin. Do not give credit to your deceitful heart. Be afraid lest self-love has blinded your eyes and hardened your heart. Pray that God will make you truly know yourself. The better thoughts you have of yourself, the worse it may be with you. The righteousness and godliness that satisfies most people is not acceptable to God. People may live forty or sixty years and yet be strangers to their hearts. We pity those in such a deluded condition, for though they seem to live in great estates, they really lie bound up in chains in a dark dungeon. Such spiritual madness impacts most people. They have never searched to the bottom of the filth in themselves. They call themselves grapes and figs when they are really thorns and thistles.

7. *The soul of man works in two ways: direct acts and reflex acts of faith.* It is a direct act when the soul by faith

directly takes Christ and clings to Him. In a reflex act, a person perceives and discerns a direct act of faith in himself. Thus when I perceive that I adhere to Christ, I discover that I love God. Certainty or assurance is properly a reflex act, in which we know that we believe. It is sometimes called *sensus fidei*, that is, the feeling or perception of faith.

Now you must know that this feeling or perceiving of faith is from God's Spirit as well as is faith itself. It is not a mere human sense, which is subject to falsehoods and delusions, but is infallible, even as faith is, for the Spirit of God cannot externally give witness to anything that is false. Neither can it work in the soul of a man to persuade him of what is not true. So, though a man may have probable hopes and conjectures of grace in his heart, he cannot be assured of that unless the Spirit of God corroborates it in him.

8. *A believer's assurance cannot be known by or demonstrated to another.* Assurance remains inexpressible in a believer's own heart. No one can truly describe what it feels like to be a father or mother to someone who has never known the experience. Similarly, when a man becomes persuaded of the truth of grace in his own soul (as differing from what a hypocrite feels), this cannot be known by another. Only the man himself may rest satisfied. He has been given the white stone that no one but he knows about.

Neither can others judge a person's certainty of faith, but we must use the judgment of charity. Only God knows the heart, and nothing is visible in a Christian that a hypocrite may not imitate upon false grounds. If some men in early times could perceive what was in a man's heart, that was by a peculiar extraordinary revelation, not by customary discerning. And that gift of discerning, which was given to some in the church, applied to distinguishing true doctrines from false. It did not discern men's hearts and affections. This is to be observed against that error which some hold, saying that a man may know whether another is godly.

Peter was initially deceived about Simon Magus, and he calls Sylvanus a faithful brother in 1 Peter 5:12. It is true that there is a great sympathy and conformable working of God's Spirit in godly men, and their hearts answer one another as the face in a mirror. Yet this discernment is not infallible, and many whom the godly have admired as stars have fallen from heaven, while others whom they did not expect to be true believers have remained firm to God.

9. *In all acts of faith (whether direct or reflex acts), the firmness and certainty of assurance depends more on God's Spirit confirming our faith than in the clearness of the argument.* Assurance consists more of the firm adhesion of the subject than in the evidence of the object. If you consider assurance as those assertive acts of faith

whereby we believe truths revealed in Scripture, then their firmness and immovableness depend more on the work of God's Spirit strengthening the inward man than upon his arguments for faith. Hence a man may continue to believe even unto martyrdom, though he is unable to answer all the objections brought against his faith. In his reflex acts of faith, the confidence that a believer has of the truth of grace wrought in him comes more from God's Spirit removing his slavish fears and disposition and supporting the soul than it does from the excellence and beauty of grace within him.

10. Just as a man rationally perceives the motions of his soul, a believer supernaturally feels the motions of his spiritual life. First John 3:14 says, "We know that we have passed from death unto life, because we love the brethren." This text teaches us two truths. The first is a general truth: those who love the brethren are translated from death to life. Second, and more particularly, it says that we who love the brethren *know* that we are translated from death to life. As a person who has fire in his bosom feels the heat, so too the person who loves God feels the motions of love within him. Just as a man perceives the motions of physical sense within him, so too a man who is spiritual feels the supernatural motions of heavenly life within him. The only difference is that a man may discern what is bitter from sweet and what is white from black without temptation or opposition, but that is not true of supernatural motions.

11. It is vain to distinguish between the certainty of hope and the certainty of faith. A person cannot have a hope of grace and godliness that is certain and not have certainty of faith. The firmness of hope depends upon the certainty of faith, so if a person has no certainty of faith, he cannot have any firmness of hope. It is true that he may strongly desire what he is not certain of by faith, but that desire cannot be the divine hope which makes us not ashamed because it is the fruit of faith that is built upon the promise and Word of God. What certainty faith has is transmitted to hope, for God has placed the natural affection of hope in man to shore him up against all the difficulties he encounters when obtaining the good he desires. God has also placed supernatural hope in the heart to support the soul until it obtains all the good things it trusts it possesses.

12. Scripture uses many words to speak of assurance. In Romans 8:38–39, the apostle Paul says he is *persuaded* that neither death nor life, neither angels nor demons, neither the present nor the future, nor any powers will be able to separate us from the love of God that is in Christ Jesus our Lord. Although the word *persuaded* may refer to either a moral or conjectural persuasion, Paul uses it here to describe the result of true faith in believers (see Rom. 15:14; Gal. 5:10). By faith Paul is confident that he will not be separated from God, but he also has confidence in the doctrines of religion. He says he "knows" whom he has believed and is "persuaded" that he is able to keep that which has been committed to him against that day (see 2 Tim. 1:12). What is more, the words that lead to Romans 8:38 are, "Who shall separate us from the love of Christ?" Ephesians 3:12 also tells us that faith is the root of the knowledge that leads to confidence, but the word that the Scripture most uses to explain it is *persuaded* (see also Rom. 4:21; Rom. 14:14; Col. 2:2; Heb. 6:11). It is used in an ill sense in Ecclesiastes 8 to say the prophet is not persuaded by wicked men.

CHAPTER 5

The Adjuncts of Assurance

Let us now add two more propositions that declare the nature of the truth that a godly man may be certain of the grace wrought in him. But first, let us note two propositions about certainty that are confounded by some divines and accurately distinguished by others.

Two Propositions
Faith Does Not Necessarily Mean Assurance
The terms *fides*, *fiducia*, and *certitude* are translated as faith, confidence, and assurance. Many writers carelessly say these words refer to the same thing. Yes, many learned men define faith as the full persuasion of the heart. They say this out of the good intention of combating the Roman Catholic emphasis on doubt. Yet it is not true. Faith does not necessarily mean assurance, for many believers have faith, even justifying faith, while having no assurance of it. That dilemma has plunged many tender consciences into sad labyrinths as if they

had no faith at all because they had no assurance. But we will discuss this further later on.

Others speak more distinctly about the distinctions between faith and assurance, often referring to Ephesians 3:11–12, which says that faith in Christ has three effects: confidence, boldness or assurance, and access to God in times of adversity, so that a believer is made God's favorite and (unlike Queen Esther's case) it is not against the law to go in and speak to this great king. Now, it is too subtle a dispute whether faith, confidence, and assurance differ only in degree—as in a child, a youth, and a man—or in kind. What is certain is that unless our faith goes so far as in a special manner to apply Christ to us, it cannot justify us or do us any good.

In Matthew 9 we see that others were in the crowd besides the woman with the issue of blood, but it was her touch alone that received Christ's virtue. Likewise, in the Old Testament, though many Israelites saw the brazen serpent, only those who looked solely upon the serpent were cured. Thus, though faith rests upon the truth of the entire Word of God, yet only truth that is applied and rests upon Christ alone justifies us.

Let not then a gracious heart despair as if it had no interest in Christ because it has not yet attained assurance. God has begun a work in you to make you desire Christ. He who supports you despite your fears and guilt will in due time give you assurance. For God bestows such mercies by degrees, even as Boaz did to

Ruth: he first gave her gleanings, then meals, and lastly himself. God may come to you in mighty rushing winds before He comes to you in a still, quiet voice. Nothing is so certain as that which follows doubt. As the shaking of trees by mighty winds makes their roots firm, so God may use temptations as a foundation of greater joy and boldness.

Assurance of Faith Does Not Eliminate All Doubt

The assurance that God's people have of their state of grace is not so high and full that it excludes all doubt, for there is nothing perfect in us in this life, whether it be our duties or our consolations. The flesh lusts against the Spirit in the work of sanctification as well as in consolation. For example, David's psalms sometimes reveal his confidence and assurance while at other times show his dejection and diffidence. Samson with his hair grown and his hair cut did not differ in strength and weakness any more than David did!

We do not therefore plead for a doctrine of assurance that excludes all doubts, all conflicts, and all agonies, such as what is experienced by the glorified saints in heaven. We have no such certainty, for our assurance is grievously assaulted by Satan, the prince of darkness, and by the unbelief of our own hearts. Though we say doubting is a grievous sin, it cannot be avoided because of the corruption that is still in us. The truth that has become a maxim in practical divinity and is grounded upon

Scripture is this: he who has never doubted has never believed, just like the one who says he is not proud has, in truth, never been humble. The ground of this truth is the fact that the fountain of sin is still flowing in every man.

Man can perform no duty or partake of any comfort without the dregs of corruption, for the leaven of sin sours both. There is some gall in all our honey, and by this means godly assurance (as is to be showed) does differ from the carnal confidence and presumption of wicked men. We may justly ask what Isaac asked Jacob when he brought his counterfeit venison, "How is it that thou hast found it so quickly, my son?" (Gen. 27:20).

The land of Canaan is not so easily possessed. The Egyptians showed this by oppressing the Israelites after they had escaped from bondage. Likewise, the devil most buffets and assaults those who have escaped his snares. As the trees that are fullest of fruit have their boughs most broken, so the people of God who carry the richest treasures of God's grace have the greatest encounters with Satan. We read about how the devil tempted Christ by asking Him to prove whether He was the Son of God. It is no wonder, then, that the devil frequently tests your strength and comfort.

Besides this, failing in our duties is a ground of coming short in our comforts. Hence the most active Christian has the greatest comfort, and he that walks loosely and lazily is fullest of doubt, just as waters that run swiftly breed no vermin or croaking frogs, but only those waters that are sluggish and stagnant.

The Adjuncts of Assurance

Before we come to practical questions about this assurance of grace, we will consider these adjuncts of it: its possibility, necessity, difficulty, and excellency.

The Possibility of Assurance

First, the possibility of assurance is seen in the people of God who have enjoyed it. When David so often calls God his God and his portion, acknowledging with joy and thankfulness that his sins have been forgiven, does not this suppose certainty? When the apostle Paul cried, "O Lord, I believe," did he speak of what he did not know? How often that apostle manifested such assurance! Lest some might think he had assurance by some special revelation, Paul in Romans 8 infers this assurance from grounds that are common to all the people of God. Therefore we cannot think such assurance impossible, saying, "I can know for sure only if those who go up to heaven bring the revelation to me that God is my God." The people of God have always found assurance in the same ways.

Second, the possibility of assurance is seen by the fact that a man may be assured of his dogmatic faith. If he believes such principles of religion upon a divine ground, why may he also not love God and His children out of true motives, since his repentance has the true ingredients? If a man could not tell whether he believed based on supernatural grounds, he could not venture to say that he believed in God indeed or that there is a church of God or a resurrection of our bodies.

Third, the possibility of assurance appears from the institution of the sacraments, which are signs and seals of God's love to us. These seals of God's love for men argue the intent of making bargains and contracts sure. God appoints sacraments as a visible, particular application, hereby declaring His will that His children should be sure of their salvation. Thus, to overthrow assurance is to take away the sacraments. As a man prizes the wax that seals his inheritance more than all the wax in the world, so Christians prize the bread and wine that is consecrated and set apart to seal the benefits of Christ to them more than all other bread and wine.

Lastly, if assurance were not possible, the defect would either be in the object, or in the means to attaining it, or in the subject. The object can have no defect, for God's promises are in Christ, yea and amen; no iota or tittle of God's promises in His Word can pass away, even in the preceptive or threatening part of them. There can be no defect in the means to obtain this assurance, either, for the Spirit of God works this grace in us. He works this through sacraments that are appointed to confirm us and through ministers who instruct us about it.

Neither is there any defect in the subject, for even though the heart of a man is so naturally deceitful and full of crafty wickedness that Scripture calls him a fool who trusts in it, yet believers are renewed by God's Spirit so that guile and hypocrisy are in great measure removed from them. A believer does not see and discern this merely in his own strength, but through the Spirit of God who enables and guides him. Thus, just as God's Spirit works by the law to convince a man of his sins, then fills him with despair of himself and everything he does, making him see he is undone and a lost man, so the same Spirit through the promise of the gospel persuades us of God's love, revealing it outwardly in the Word and inwardly in our hearts.

The Necessity of Assurance

We know that assurance is necessary, first, because of the nature of faith. Assurance is of an establishing and settling nature. It is a pillar and an anchor to the soul. Though assurance is separable from faith, yet Scripture clearly says that doubts and fears are the opposite of believing. Trusting in God is compared to rolling ourselves upon Him, to staying our minds, and to resting our hearts. So by strong and customary acts of believing in Christ and patiently waiting, we come at last to be assured.

Second, assurance is necessary because it is part of God's glory. It is not enough that God works grace in us and sanctifies us. We must also know it, that we may praise and bless God for it. Can a man in his sleep, in a swoon, or when his senses are stupefied praise God that he lives? He cannot any more than a Christian who staggers with uncertainties and darkness of mind. How it should quicken us, then, to obtain the mercy of assurance! How much glory God loses by our fears! As David argued, how can the dead praise God? So you too may ask, "O LORD, how can those in darkness with no light glorify Thee for Thy goodness to them?"

Third, assurance is necessary because it gives us more joy and peace in our hearts. Oh, what hell must a man experience who has not even a little light of this assurance in his soul? What legions of doubts must torment him till he has some measure of assurance? How can a man be sick, in danger, or under the stroke of death without any knowledge of any good that God has wrought in him? Hezekiah in his sickness rested in the Lord for assurance, saying, "Remember, O LORD, how I have walked before thee with a true heart." Likewise, Paul was animated to look death in the face because he had fought a good fight. Is not that the argument today of many who languish on their deathbeds? If a dying person had such assurance, how willingly could he depart from this world!

Fourth, assurance is necessary because it enlarges and quickens us to perform holy duties. A person with this hope purifies himself, even as God is pure (1 John 3:3). With the promises of God being our God and we

His people, let us cleanse ourselves from all filthiness of self and spirit, says the apostle Paul in 2 Corinthians 7:1. We believe; therefore we speak. It is thus an opinion against manifest existence that the assurance of God's love will promote presumption and carnal security. Assurance is like fire in our bowels or wings to our soul. Does not a child who is assured that his father loves him become more willing and ready to obey? Is not this a beautiful epigram from the poet Martial, "If you want to be loved, love!" When a believer is persuaded that God in great love has worked such mercies for him, will not this make him seven times more enflamed by God?

The Difficulty of Assurance

We know that it is difficult for a believer to have assurance of salvation, and that few possess it, because of the following reasons.

First, when a person senses and feels the guilt of sin, he may initially look upon God as an enemy, who, like a human, cannot forgive but will certainly avenge. Think of Cain and Judas, for example, and how prone they were to despair after they had grievously sinned. Therefore the word for *assure* in 1 John 3:19 signifies persuasion, implying that our hearts have many peevish objections that must be overcome. Like Rachel mourning for her children, we are not easily comforted.

Second, the difficulty of obtaining assurances arises from the desperate hypocrisy and falseness of our hearts. Roman Catholics argue this truth to the point of declaring that the Spirit of God is incapable of providing us with assurance, but we know otherwise. Though assurance is not a flower that naturally grows in our garden, the Spirit does work grace in us and gives us eyes to discern it so that we should not remain in darkness.

Third, the difficulty of obtaining assurance arises from our proneness to walk negligently and carelessly. We are beaten down with many temptations and therefore quickly lose hope; for assurance is preserved only in the continual exercise of grace. The apostle Peter tells us to be diligent to make our calling and election sure (2 Peter 1:10), implying that if we do not walk carefully, using all the means of grace that God has given us, we cannot obtain the warmth of assurance, but will remain in coldness. Does not this lukewarmness, earthliness, and coldness grieve the Spirit of God who would seal us?

Fourth, assurance is difficult because of causes outside of the believer, including both Satan and God. Satan, who has fiery darts, has been a manslayer from the beginning. He endeavors to keep us in doubts and fears so that we may eventually become so weary that we rage against God. When the devil cannot hinder us in our duties, he works to minimize our comforts and consolations, for as the Spirit of God brings comfort to the people of God, so the devil is the tempter who waits for any opportunity to throw bitter wormwood into every condition we are in. He is like the pirates who wait to attack ships that are full of gold and other treasures. He does not bother wicked men to cast them down with fears and troubles, for they do not know either the meaning of spiritual temptations or what it is to have the light of God's countenance denied them. No, his target is the godly man who struggles for assurance.

On God's part, He makes assurance difficult to obtain so that His favor may be more prized. The church that carelessly puts off her Beloved, then afterwards makes a great and vehement inquiry after Christ often cannot find Him. Though God does not withhold assurance of faith to make us careless and negligent, yet sometimes He does this so that the blessing is not abused through our corruption.

The Excellency of Assurance

The privilege of assurance is excellent for the following reasons.

First, assurance allows us to have excellent fellowship and acquaintance with God. The church that can say, "I am my beloved's, and my beloved is mine" (Song of Songs 6:3), abounds in spiritual community with Christ. This expression is used four or five times in Scripture. In contrast to assurance, fears and doubts keep us aloof from Christ and make us slavishly tremble before Him.

Second, assurance produces a filial and evangelical frame of heart. The spirit of adoption that enables us to call God our Father also gives us the humble disposition of sons, enabling us to serve Him from pure intentions and motives.

Third, assurance will support us even when we are experiencing nothing but outward misery and trouble. In those times when we cannot be assured of anything, such as our homes, safety, or lives, assurance of God's grace worked in our souls will be a wall of marble that cannot be beaten down. With such assurance, Paul triumphed over all difficulties in his life (Romans 8).

Fourth, assurance of God's love will motivate us to pray. Prayer kindles desires, increases hope, and makes the soul more importunate. David often encouraged himself in prayer. If experience breeds hope, much more will assurance.

Fifth, assurance makes a man walk with much tenderness against sin, for such evil would put him out of the heaven of experiencing how sweet the Lord is and how greatly His favor is to be prized. He will take heed that he does not rob himself of so great a treasure. Why do men fear to displease those who can do what they will, keeping all earthly evidences of faith from them? Should we not rather seek to please God, who can deny us our heavenly evidence of faith?

Sixth, assurance makes a man impatient and earnest for the return of Christ. "I desire to depart," says Paul, "and to be with Christ, where I shall have a full possession and accomplishment of all glory." If the beginnings of assurance in this life are so wonderful and excellent, what will heaven itself be like, where all fears are abandoned! Seneca said of his wise man, "He is more in heaven than on earth." This is even truer of the godly who have assurance of faith.

Seventh, a full acquiescence to and resting in God and Christ are sufficient to meet every need, so that they desire nothing in heaven but Christ and nothing on earth besides Him. Having drunk of this living water they thirst no more, but all their happiness is in Christ. Blessed is the man who has partaken of the privilege of assurance, and happy is he who in this manner has God for his God, and Christ for his Christ!

CHAPTER 6

The Difference between True Assurance and Presumption

We will now consider more precisely the distinct differences between assurance and presumption. You have heard that the greatest delusion and madness that can be is to have a persuasion of our state as sound and godly when the opposite is true. Yet the majority of Christians possess such carnal confidence. They are like the mad Athenian who thought all the ships on the sea were his. How many there are who when they hear of the precise evidences of grace conclude that they are presently shut out of God's kingdom, yet they do bless themselves as if all were well with them! It is therefore worthwhile to ransack such false evidences in order to discover the differences between dross and gold, honey and gall, and what is of the flesh and what is of the Spirit.

Differences in the Causes of True Assurance and Presumption

There is a vast difference between the efficient causes or principles of true assurance and presumption. Though causes are like roots under the ground that are not so visible, they are critical to what they produce. Assurance is a fruit that has its roots in heaven. The Spirit of God works a twofold act, enlightening or revealing, and adopting or corroborating the heart with filial evangelical affections. By contrast, carnal presumption is like a rush plant that grows in the mire of our own hearts. The internal causes that give life and breath to presumption include the following.

Ignorance and Inexperienced Apprehension of the Death and Danger of Sin

Unlike Paul, such people have not yet found the law of God alive and themselves dead. They have not truly seen the great abominations of their nature, the foulness of sin, the purity of the law, and the exactness of God's justice. Since they lack these discoveries and apprehensions, they are quickly persuaded that everything is well with their souls.

That was the case with Paul prior to his conversion. He thought he was spiritually alive and had great confidence in himself. This in general was the state of the Pharisees, who justified themselves, and of the Jews, who trusted in their own righteousness. There was no ground for such confidence except that these men were blind and ignorant and did not truly know themselves. They were like the Laodiceans who thought themselves rich and full while they were actually poor and miserable.

Thus the presumption of unregenerate men arises from stupidity and blindness, whereas godly assurance is wrought out of gracious illumination about the height, depth, and breadth of sin, with a tender affection about the weight and burden of it. Do you presume the love of God and rest upon the goodness of your heart? If you were truly acquainted with all the wounds sin has made upon you, if your eyes were opened to perceive the filth and vileness of your nature and ways, you would sit like Job upon a dunghill, abhorring and loathing yourself.

Self-Love

Another internal cause of presumption is self-love. The ivy of self-love cleaves closer and closer to us until it devours our substance. With such self-love we flatter ourselves, assuming that everything within us is good when it is altogether filthy and carnal. The wise man observes that every man's ways are clean in his own eyes, but God ponders the heart. As it is said, whoever excuses and acquits himself, accuses himself before God. This was the epidemic disease of the Jews, for what prophet could persuade them that their hearts were not right with God? Who could bring them out of love with themselves?

Are you fully persuaded of your good state before God? Do you bless God for your good heart and affections? What is the ground of this? Is it from self-flattery and carnal love for yourself? If you were truly diligent and observant, you would discover the real ground of your carnal confidence. Godly assurance arises from utter loathing of our sinful souls.

Differences in the Motives and Grounds of True Assurance and Presumption

A second vast difference between true assurance and presumption is evident in their motives and grounds. Godly assurance comes through the Word of God. In other words, the means of our regeneration is also the means of our assurance. The apostle Paul says in 2 Corinthians 1 that the Scriptures are given to us so we may have comfort, whereas vain presumption comes from base and unworthy motives, which include the following.

Mere Natural Light and Judgment about the State of Regeneration and Grace

True assurance comes to us by the light of the Spirit shining through God's Word. The work of grace in our hearts cannot be discerned by natural light any more than the physical senses can apprehend the actions and work of reason or the natural faculty of the will to do what is supernaturally good.

Nicodemus is a good example of how blind we can be about the work of regeneration. This is the motive of most people's assurance: their gross mistake about the nature of the work of grace. Do not most people think that godliness is consistent with frequent and constant acts of impiety and daily neglect of holy duties? How many say they have a good heart, notwithstanding their bad tongues and lives? If they are not so gross as to be deluded with this, do not many assume that fair, civil, and moral conversation, void of scandal, is the essence of scriptural godliness, and, because they have this kind of conversation, they are therefore persuaded they possess a godly condition?

A man's mistake may be even greater, such as when he takes a working of God's Spirit which was but for a season or was in some ways imperfect or of shorter degrees, and not truly rooted in the soul, and believes it to be the peculiar saving work of grace which is in the truly regenerated only. It is easy to be deceived by such mistaken notions and, like the foolish virgins in Matthew 25, to boldly approach the Bridegroom when our lamps have run out of oil. Therefore, examine yourself to see if the motive of your assurance is not mistaken about the nature of sanctifying grace.

Worth, Merit, or Perfection We Deem in Ourselves

The motives of a godly assurance are not from any worth, merit, or perfection we imagine in ourselves, but only from the truth and sincerity of grace, with many defects that are washed away by Christ's blood. Though the apostle Paul was not aware of any defect in himself, he was not thereby justified. Therefore the Roman

Catholic description of hope, arising partly from the merits of Christ and partly from our own merits, is a bold presumption. We do not defend the assurance that arises from full and perfect obedience to God's law, either, for such obedience is impossible in this life. We may only have a certain persuasion of the uprightness of our hearts in the ways of God. The Roman Catholics militate against assurance chiefly upon this ground because no one can say he has a clean heart, and that in many ways we sin. These truths do indeed argue strongly against a perfection in this life, but not against a gracious assurance.

The Outward Comforts and Plenty We Enjoy

Many Christians look upon their riches, children, and honors as testimonies of God's love to them and as rewards for their obedience. Because Scripture offers so many temporal promises to those who walk in God's ways, those who find themselves blessed thus infer their piety. But Scripture includes many antidotes against this tumor and swelling, telling us that such people stand in slippery places spiritually, for such things may become a snare to us, increasing both our sin and torment. Augustine said that Solomon also observed that riches can hurt those who have them. As he says in Ecclesiastes, no man knows love or hatred because of outward riches. This does not mean, as the Roman Catholics would have it, that no assurance is possible at all. It simply means that we may have no assurance by mere outward mercies and favors. The rich man received his good things in this life, while Lazarus received evil things.

Actually, genuine assurance is most powerful and operative in the midst of outward distresses and miseries. Consider how David in some of his psalms expressed his confidence in God, though outward things seemed to indicate that God was against him. Likewise Hezekiah, when confronted by the stroke of death, was supported with the truth of grace in his soul. Carnal confidence vanishes in times of distress. People without genuine assurance rage and rave in times of trouble, not knowing what to do. What keeps up your spirit? Is it your wealth or possessions? Alas, how things are given so many times to those whom God hates. But if outward things contribute to happiness, then Christ was not happy, for He became poor that we might be rich.

Augustine rightly observed that God sometimes gives riches to wicked men so that we may not think outward things are good in themselves. And sometimes He gives riches to godly men so that we may not think outward things evil in themselves. God may give you many things, and not Christ; but if He gives you Christ, how shall He not with Him give us all else?

Differences in the Manners and Methods of True Assurance and Presumption

Though the wind blows where it wills and God's ways vary among His people, yet the hearts of God's people ordinarily come to assurance through the Spirit's work in similar ways. The shared experience of the faithful, though not expressly described in Scripture, can still contain sober authority. Here are some of the ways in which God brings assurance to believers.

By a Deep and Serious Humiliation and Burden over Sin

Matthew 11 tells us that only those who have been humbled deeply before God because of their sins can find rest in their souls. Christ did not assure Mary Magdalene that her sins were forgiven until after she had wept much for them. We do not specify the amount of time or the degree of humiliation, only the necessity of it, before a sinner can embrace true assurance. So when we meet a person who is confident that it is well with his soul, we know what travails his soul must have suffered before he could have such joy. Romans 8 tells us that the Spirit of God is a Spirit of bondage before He is a Spirit of adoption. That is enough to shake the foundation of many men's buildings. What deep digging was there in your heart before you found assurance?

This true and safe practical divinity is rejected by some people who turn religion into notions and opinions. But in Romans 7 and 8, Paul describes how his soul was brought to assurance in this way. He says he first discovered his true condition through the law, whereby he judged himself miserable and out of measure sinful. Then he came to see the apprehension of Christ's grace upon him. True assurance will not grow upon a heart that is not first plowed up. The needle must pierce the heart before silk can follow.

By Doubts and Unbelief

God also works assurance by inner conflicts with doubt and opposition against unbelief. Seeing that assurance is a fruit of God's Spirit while doubting is a work of the flesh, the apostle's rule is verified that the flesh wars against the spirit and the spirit against the flesh. I do not trust an assurance that never doubted. It is like the conviction of the rich young ruler who said he has kept the law of God from the time he was a youth. It is inconceivable that so great and spiritual a mercy should be brought into sinners without any struggles. It is always a good sign when apprehensions of grace in us are often accompanied by feelings of our imperfections, even as the father of the demon-possessed son prayed in Mark 9:24, "Lord, I believe" (which demonstrates the assurance of grace in him); "help thou mine unbelief" (which demonstrates his perception of his defects in faith). Likewise the psalmist David sometimes testifies of the sunshine of God's favor, at which time everything is clear for his own soul, while at other times he is in the dark and wavers much.

Through the Vehement and Fiery Assaults of Satan
As Christ Himself did not escape the arrows of Satan, neither do the members of His body. Woe, then, to the man whose peace the devil does not disrupt. The strong one, who is the devil, kept all things subdued till the stronger one, Christ, came. As the basilisk, a legendary reptile said to be able to kill people with a single glance, hates the very picture of a man, so the devil opposes the resemblance of Christ. Think, therefore, that vain presumption rather than godly assurance is not opposed by hell itself. He is an Egyptian, not an Israelite, if Pharaoh does not oppress him.

Differences in the Effects of Godly Assurance and Presumption
A fourth difference between godly assurance and presumption is in the effects whereby godly assurance outstrips presumption as light outshines darkness. They include the following.

Diligent in the Use of the Means and Careful to Perform All Duties
The neglect of these means causes assurance to either perish or weaken. Thus, as the apostle Peter says, give all diligence to make your calling and election sure (2 Peter 1:10). When diligence is not fully pursued, there is no assurance. Diligence is the oil that keeps the lamp

burning, for earnest prayer, the holy use of sacraments, and walking universally in all God's ways maintain this godly certainty. Carnal confidence, on the other hand, is big and swells even in the neglect or profane contempt of the means. A man who does not pray and who pollutes himself with daily sins can thus be thoroughly persuaded of his happiness. Yet in the ordinary passages of God's providence this man is rightly judged a presumer, who persuades himself of life when he will neither eat nor drink or be assured of wealth and riches when he fails to be diligent. This arrogant insobriety is evident in a spiritual presumer.

The Greater Assurance Is, the More It Enflames the Heart with Love for God

True assurance is like a burning glass, which, by reflecting a sunbeam, will kindle a fire, as we told you of David and Paul. And none do so highly bless God and praise Him as those who have this assurance, whereas the effects of carnal presumption are love of the creature or the comforts he enjoys, while caring little for God. The more confident an adulteress is of her husband's love, the bolder and more impudent she is to abuse it. But the Spirit of adoption bestows a filial disposition. Assurance of the Father's love melts the believer into a filial frame of heart. But if love is shown to a slavish spirit, it makes this spirit more haughty and lofty. Consider, therefore, how assurance works in you. Does it extinguish all your love for sin and the world? Does it kill your inordinate affections for things below and raise your heart to God so that you delight and rejoice in Him? This is a comfortable demonstration of good assurance.

Potent and Able to Lift the Heart above All Discouragements and Desolations

When David was most oppressed, he found encouragement in the Lord his God (1 Sam. 30:6). This certainty of our propriety and interest in God is an ark for the soul in the midst of many waters, whereas the heart of a carnally confident man becomes like a stone within him when all carnal hopes fail. Godly assurance is a precious symptom in the midst of the confusions we live in. When heaven and earth seem to be mingled together, what else can make you rejoice and lift up your head with gladness? Is it not the knowledge you have God to be your God? Is it not those pledges and pawns in your soul of His eternal love and goodness to you? Such things are substantial.

Sadly, hypocrites have joy, but their confidence quickly perishes. Their joy is not a star fixed in the orb of quintessential matter, but is a blazing star compiled of slimy material that will quickly be consumed and vanish away. Origen said that true assurance is like a metal that is under trial; if it can endure the blows of the hammer above it and the anvil below it yet continue to be inflexible, then it is true metal. So it is with true assurance. It abides despite the billows and waves that seek to overcome it. Therefore, troubles will discern the truth of your graces and comforts better than anything else. Hence, as Richard Cameron (1648–1680) observed, mercies are not called temptations in Scripture, but rather *afflictions* because it is so difficult to be deprived of what we desire.

Differences in the Companions of True Assurance and Presumption

There is a palpable difference in the companions and concerns of true assurance, which include the following.

Holy Fear and Trembling

God's Word does not contradict itself. In some places it asks us to make our calling sure and in other places to work out our salvation with fear and trembling. These two graces do not contradict one another, for the subject is the same. Thus those who are assured may rejoice, yet do so with fear and trembling. Those who are assured shall stand, yet take heed lest they fall. A man who holds onto battlements knows he cannot fall, yet when he looks down to ground that is so far below him, he cannot help but fear that he might fall. Thus at the same time he has both the assurance of not falling and the fear of falling, though not from the same considerations. It is not so with those in whom carnal presumptions exclude all kinds of fear and obstruct all diligence.

Humility and Lowliness of Mind

The greater the mercies are that God bestows upon His people, the lowlier they are in their own eyes. For example, the Virgin Mary testifies of God's grace to her, a humble servant, while David writes psalms to describe God's kindness to a lowly shepherd boy. By contrast, in carnal presumption, the more confidence a person has, the more prideful he becomes of himself and the more disdainful of others.

How might we prove that a Pharisee did not have assurance of grace in him, but by his vain confidence? The Pharisee despises other men as sinners compared to himself. This may make us justly doubt whether those who speak of the immediate revelations and assurances they have from God's Spirit are not pridefully deluded by condemning others as below themselves and not truly acquainted with God's Spirit. For there is such a danger of pride even in godly men who are lifted up to great privileges as Paul was in experiencing the third heaven before he was assaulted with the buffetings of Satan. Twice he explained in 2 Corinthians 12:7 why he had to endure a "thorn in the flesh": "Lest I should be exalted above measure," in the beginning of the verse and, again, "Lest I should be exalted," at the end of the verse. This temptation of Satan exercising Paul in the midst of his revelations may be compared to the boy who as a monitor cried aloud to a soldier riding in triumph, "Remember thyself to be a man."

If pride is a danger even in godly men who have in them the true works of God's Spirit, what is the cause of pride in corrupted men who have only infected delusions of Satan? When your persuasion of God's love to you raises such lofty mountains in your soul that you consider yourself to be in heaven while others grovel upon the ground, when you deem yourself to be as much above other Christians as an angel is above a worm, then be afraid, for the devil often transforms himself into an angel of light.

Differences in the Opposites of True Assurance and Presumption

Lastly, true assurance differs from what is opposite to it and will destroy it. Assurance is wrought by God's Spirit and is only interrupted by sin, so grieve not the Spirit of God by whom you are sealed. Corrupt and idle communication, or little sins (as the world judges), may greatly disturb our certainty, whereas carnal presumption is not weakened by sin. Only outward troubles or horrors of confidence vanquish presumption. There is a difference between depression and a troubled conscience for sin, for depression may often be removed by bodily remedies, joyful company, and various activities, whereas a troubled conscience can only be eased by comforts from Scripture. Though Cain traveled and built cities, he could not free himself from guilt that trembled within him. On the contrary, peace in the

Holy Spirit worked by assurance is only excluded by sin or lukewarmness in holy duties, whereas sinful confidence is not removed until it is shaken or removed by some outward troubles.

CHAPTER 7

Remedies for Carnal Confidence and Directions to the Godly Who Lack Assurance

Having declared the differences between carnal presumption and godly assurance, let us now consider what engines are needed to batter down the strongholds into which the carnally confident man has fled, and what must be said to undeceive him and put him in the way of salvation.

First, however, let us examine the truth that no one has higher mountains and hills to overcome than a falsely deluded Christian, for no one is more indisposed for Christ. Christ told the Pharisees that publicans and harlots would reach heaven before they did, confirming the saying that a disease that most resembles health is often the most difficult to cure. Likewise, the task is greater to remove a deluded Christian from his steadfastness in presumption because two things must be done: he must be convinced that the righteousness he is persuaded of is false, and he must be convinced of the true righteousness that leads to assurance.

A philosopher who was asked to teach a student infected with false opinions demanded a double fee because he had to unteach the false opinions before he could teach true ones. Likewise, the prophets of God were tasked with double teaching. Jesus Christ, who had the tongue of the learned, spoke in parables to make the full hungry and to empty the rich of themselves.

What the heretic is in doctrine, the carnal presumer is in matters of practice and conversation. Now the former is seldom reduced because a presumer is obstinate against all admonitions, and the latter is scarcely ever truly debased and humbled because of the self-love that cleaves to him.

Remedies against Carnal Confidence
If anything is able to overrule and conquer carnal confidence, the following remedies are most likely to do it.

A Powerful and Soul-Searching Ministry
This kind of ministry will pierce into a man to expose the hidden things of his heart so that he may come to truly know himself. The ministry of the word is like the sun in the firmament, from whose light nothing is hidden. The Old Testament prophets and the New Testament apostles were lights. What convictions might the Jews have had of their self-centeredness and hypocrisies if they had not shut their eyes against these lights?

The weapons of ministry are mighty in pulling down worldly strongholds and everything that exalts itself, meaning all kinds of opposition (2 Cor. 10:4–5). The woman of Samaria said that Christ knew everything she had done. Like her, we may sometimes cry out to others, "Come and hear a sermon that has exposed all the vileness, inward filthiness, poverty, and wretchedness that is within me!"

The Opening and Applying of the Law In Its Purity and Rigidity

What an excellent course our Savior takes in Matthew 5 to make listeners afraid of themselves and to see more sins in themselves than they ever thought of! He makes the law so spiritual and so deeply penetrating in reaching into all the motions and lusts of the soul that they must be as foul as black moors in God's eyes, even while sinners admire their own beauty. You bless yourself because of the innocence in your outward conversation and your freedom from gross sins, but no dunghill is fuller of snakes and worms than your heart is of filthy lusts. Thus, in Romans 7 Paul says that as good as he was in his own eyes, he found that as he looked into the mirror of God's Word, His holy law, he found so many blots and blemishes in himself that he no longer had life or hope within him. Hence those who keep themselves from appearing as deformed as they truly are limit the sense of the law, as if it were not as penetrating as it is. They are like the elephant that muddies the water so that it may not see its own deformity.

Discovering the Necessity and Fullness of Christ

If Christ is so necessary, as Scripture says, that His righteousness must be all in all, this demonstrates that all we have is sin and weakness. If Christ is commended to us as Savior, Physician, and Redeemer, then certainly we are sick, in bondage, and utterly undone in ourselves. Why, then, oh vain man, do you boast in yourself? Why are you so strongly persuaded of your own sufficiency? If that is so, what need do you have of Christ? Was He not incarnated? Did He suffer in vain? If a star could give light to the world and dispel all darkness, what need would there be of a sun? If a stream had enough water to refresh, what use would there be of the ocean? If you would become poor and miserable in your own eyes, consider the glory, riches, fullness, and absolute necessity of Christ that Scripture sets forth so that you may then quickly abhor yourself.

*Outward and Sad Afflictions Accompanying
the Word*

When God by His Word thunders in our ears and hearts, and when He outwardly scourges and afflicts us, then we are often released from our lofty imaginations. We deal honestly and forthrightly with those who have false conceits of their outward happiness because sometimes that is the only way to bring them to a true knowledge of themselves. Likewise, when God wants a man to reject all his carnal presumptions and abhor all high thoughts of himself, He hangs many weights upon the man, causing many thorns to run into his side. How much better it would be for that man to be kept by God in darkness and sad plunges of his own spirit than to be set, as it were, upon the pinnacle of the temple. Be therefore awakened out of your security, and fear, lest you have lived many years in a mere dream of your holiness and interest in Christ.

Those Who Seem to Have Made Great Progress but Have Had Dreadful Ends

Though some men have had high thoughts of themselves, their ends have been so dreadful and terrible that their examples may be a special help to rouse us out of false presumptions. Their end should be like a sword in our bowels (Hebrews 6). They had some illumination and savory taste in some degree of the goodness of God and His Word, yet they lacked those things that truly accompany salvation. They are like the foolish virgins who were bold in their preparations for the bridegroom yet found out how woefully they were deluded. Consider these examples again and again, lest their cases and yours be alike. Think and tremble lest the time come when you shall cry for oil because all yours is spent and there is no one to help you. Our Savior taught many parables to teach us how prone we are to be thus deceived.

Consider How Apt a Presumptuous Man Is to
Err in Other Things

Every man is so full of blindness, stupidity, and ignorance that it is no wonder that he is often deceived in natural and moral things as well as supernatural truths. Is it any wonder that in the working of his own heart he is commonly carried by self-love? If a natural man does not correctly perceive natural things, how can he perceive the things of God? As our Savior said, if you fail to understand earthly things, how can you understand the things of heaven? If a godly man, out of whose heart guile and hypocrisy is in a great measure removed, does yet cry out, "Who can understand my errors and cleanse me from secret sins," how much more is that true of the person who is wholly in the leaven of hypocrisy? If David had much pride and corruption in his heart, how much more has a Pharisee or an unregenerate man? William Ames (1576–1633) said that one who presumes is in the more desperate condition because he has failed to despair over his true state.

How the Godly May Find Assurance

What should a man do when he has the truth of grace in him, but has no assurance of it? Though God has wrought supernatural cures upon this man, yet he does not believe such mercy is done for him. Then, too, a man who lacks assurance of grace in his soul may also be conflicted about the assurance of election, justification, preservation, and glorification. When a soul is in darkness about the former and has no knowledge of it, he may also be ignorant about other things. While carnal men know not the sadness of such a condition, David describes this condition in his psalms in ways that make it appear most horrid. He says it is like the pain of broken bones—that is, not one broken bone, but all of them broken. How intolerable is such pain! Christ, who prayed for the light of God's favor in His agony, though no corporate bone was broken, experienced the pain of these broken bones. What should you do when you mourn under the sense that you lack God's favor?

Examine Yourself for Unrepented Sin

Unrepented sin may eclipse all the certainty of salvation. That was certainly true of David, whose unconfessed adultery drove away the spirit of gladness and joy in his soul. Oh, what joy and confidence are expelled by the committing of gross sins! How can there be assurance and peace, as if grace were in you, when you demonstrate such works of the flesh and Satan? Is it any wonder then that men who profess to be religious yet live loosely, falling repeatedly into foul sins, often wreak hell upon their consciences and frequent terrors upon their soul? When vapors are gathered together in the bowels of the earth, they cannot help but produce an earthquake; so sins gathered together in the heart will one time or another produce a heartquake. Ephesians 4 tells us not to grieve the Spirit of God. If our sin grieves the Spirit, how just is it that God's Spirit should grieve us?

See If You Have Been Negligent in the Means of Grace
If no grievous sins have created a great gulf between a believer and his assurance, he might consider whether a careless use of the means of grace has weakened his certainty. You have heard that you must give all diligence to make your calling sure, for without constant diligence this assurance cannot be obtained. Though sincere and zealous endeavors after godliness do not cause assurance, yet they are the sign and testimony of God's love, so without them there can be no comfort at all. Fervent and gracious performances of holy duties are the oil without which a lamp cannot shine. When the apostle exhorted us to prayer, saying that we should make our requests known to God, he added, "and the peace of God shall rule in your hearts." It is therefore an unworthy thing to complain about the loss of God's favor and assurance if all your duties and performances are careless and withered.

Realize That Assurance Is a Privilege God Bestows When and Where He Chooses
It is the Spirit of adoption who works that filial affection that enables us to cry, "Abba, Father." It is the Spirit of God who seals that to us. Thus assurance does not flow out of the workings of grace in us by a natural and

necessary consequence, but by the immediate application of God's love to us. Hence 2 Corinthians 1 says that God is the God of all consolation who comforts us. God does not act like a Christian friend or minister responding to one who is tempted to sin, outwardly propounding comfort and offering arguments of consolation but incapable of inwardly turning and changing his heart. Rather, God outwardly commands His people to be assured and comforted in such a way that their hearts are inwardly fashioned and formed to receive this assurance. That same power of God in converting grace is also evident in His work of consolation. God desires to teach us by this that assurance is not a flower which grows by itself in the garden of our hearts.

Understand That the Truth of Grace May Be in You Without You Being Aware of It

Hagar had a fountain of water near her in the desert, but she did not see it until God opened her eyes to it. Likewise you must continue the constant exercise of your graces. You are bound to love God, trust in Him, and perform all duties, even though your heart does not feel God's love to you. For though the assurance of God's favor is like coals of fire poured upon the soul to melt it, yet we are obliged to continue the spiritual exercise of holy duties even if God does not give us His encouragement, because to the one who overcomes He will give the hidden manna and the white stone (Rev. 2:17).

The privilege of assurance is given to those who have been acquainted with God for a long time, are much exercised in His ways, and have endured much for Him. That is not to say that God does not grant assurance at times to new converts who discover the love of His espousals to them because they are spiritually tender and need it, being much oppressed by sin. As Aristotle said, parents are often most tender to their youngest child because that child is least capable of caring for himself or herself.

Why God Does Not Grant Assurance to Those Who Have True Grace

When God has worked grace in us, why does He not always enable us to immediately believe and to see that faith in our own souls? Though David was told through the prophet that his sin was taken away, we see in Psalm 51 how earnestly David continued to pray for pardon and joy. This implies that though God caused forgiveness to be outwardly declared to David, yet He did not by His almighty power effectually persuade David of it immediately. The question why seems the greater when we consider that assurance is like wings and legs in a man's service to God. It enflames him more to promote God's glory. Besides, without it God will lose much glory and honor, for how can the soul rejoice to give God praise for the mercy which he does not know he has received? Not to know our pardon and not to have it are one in the matter of thankfulness. Yet God frequently keeps His own people in darkness. How many times are they ready with Zion to say, "God has forsaken us"? But there are several good reasons why God, though He has put grace in our souls, may delay in publishing it to our consciences.

That We May Taste and See How Bitter Sin Is

The longer guilt with its consequences is upon our souls, the greater cause we have to bewail and abominate it. If assurance was in our power to have whenever we desired, how slight and shallow would our thoughts be about sin? David's length of time under the guilt of murder and adultery wrought greater hatred and dislike of those sins in his soul. And however it may seem to be a servile low spirit to despise sin because of the bitterness of it and not only because of our love of God and delight in Him, yet no better is the spirit of the most refined and reformed godly man in this. Be therefore content under the seeming black desertions of God. Though you know not how it is with your soul, yet God's good purpose is to keep you low and weary of sin.

That God May Keep Us Low and Humble

Upon the discovery of God's works in our hearts, we are apt to grow high in self-regard and to condemn others. We are also apt to think God has raised us above others because we know and feel more of God than other men do. So God hides His face from us that all such worms of pride may be killed, that we may see nothing but our sin and weakness, and that our whole life may appear as nothing. Anselm of Canterbury (c. 1033–1109) said that we have either sin or barrenness, when our hearts see nothing but sin. Then we can lie before the throne of God, which is rich in grace, like Lazarus (who was full of sores) lay before the rich man's gate. Peter Chrysologus (c. 380–c. 450), the bishop of Ravenna, said of Lazarus that he had as many mouths crying for help as he had sores. So will you have as many mouths begging for pardon as you have sins and infirmities.

Scripture tells us that the face of Moses was so bright after being with God that the people of Israel were not able to behold it. Yet Moses was not aware of this. How excellent it is then when others can behold and admire the grace of God in you, yet you apprehend it not! Gregory said that a man ought, by not knowing to know, and by knowing not, to know the grace of God in him.

That When We Have Assurance, We More Esteem It and Take Heed As to How We Lose It

In Song of Songs we see how the woman (i.e., the church) who despised her spouse's love was so earnest to get it back again, even though it cost her much to obtain it. Seneca said that the sun is not admired until it is eclipsed. Likewise, some people do not highly esteem the favor and love of God until they fear they have lost it. As it is with temporal mercies, so spiritual mercies are prized by wanting them more than having them. Do you pray and pray for assurance, yet cannot obtain it? Then think that this delay may be meant to increase your appetite more for it, so that when your soul does enjoy it, you may bless God more.

That We May Demonstrate Obedience to God and Give Him Greater Honor

To rely upon God by faith, when you have no sensible testimonies of His love to you, is the purest and most basic act of obedience that you could offer. It is like the faith of adherence that Christ exercised in His suffering. A man may desire assurance, as it breeds peace and ease to his soul. But to depend upon God during spiritual desertions and to wholly give all to God and nothing to self is a kind of spiritual martyrdom. Assurance brings more comfort to you, while believing gives more glory to God. When Abraham did not stagger in trusting God, even though Sarah's womb was dead, he glorified God. No less is that true of your faith when you overlook your senses, feelings, and temptations and trust God for acceptance. To walk by assurance is a kind of walking by sense. It supposes that we, like children, cannot be quiet unless we know we are in our mother's bosom.

That We May Offer Comfort to Others in Distress
Christ was tempted by the wrath of God so that He might have sympathy and feeling for those who are likewise exercised. Paul says that God comforted him in his tribulations so that he might comfort others who likewise suffered. He who is not tempted about the pardon of sin may wonder about those who are so afflicted and be unable to apply fit remedies. We see carnal and natural people judging those who lack assurance as being beside themselves and distracted. They bid them enjoy worldly company, worldly feasting, and worldly entertainment, thinking carnal plaster will heal their spiritual sore. Job 33:23 describes the condition of a man being chastened for sin so that he utterly refuses all comforts and would consider it a great mercy to have a messenger show him his uprightness. This messenger he calls "one among a thousand." Therefore, make good use of such trials, for God might use them to raise us to be a Joseph to brethren in need.

May God bless these truths to destroy the foundations of carnal presumption, which is a common sin and damns thousands. Indeed, presumption is a more grievous sin than despair, for in despair a man is weary of himself, abhors his condition, and would if he could admit better counsel, while a presumer pleases himself and will not hearken to any good admonitions. Oh, how sadly you are deluded and how frustrated your expectations will be when you see nothing but hell and confusion instead of the joy and comfort you promised yourself! The foolish virgins saw their oil was gone when it was too late to do anything about it. Do you also fear lest you are plunged into such horrid extremities? The nearer you are to the haven of heaven when you suffer shipwreck, the more lamentable it is. The church's complaint, "We looked for peace, but behold, trouble," accentuates her misery.

CHAPTER 8

Marks of Grace and Assurance

We now come to the second part of this doctrine, which is that there are signs of grace whereby a man may know whether he is in the state of grace. It is a point worth discussing because many people criticize ministers who preach about signs of grace and discourage Christians from using those signs to examine themselves. It is also necessary because much prudence is required in the minister when preaching about these signs. And the Christian must carefully consider these marks—which is an art of arts—without splitting himself upon some rock or other. So that we may discover the truth of this entire doctrine, let us first consider these introductory particulars about assurance.

By the Inherent Grace of Sanctification We Come to Have a Supernatural Being

Through the grace of sanctification, we come to have a supernatural being. As natural things have a natural being because of the natural form that is in them, so the godly have a supernatural being because of the infused principle of a holy life in them. As 1 Peter 1:4 says, we become partakers of the divine nature. A regenerated man is called a new creature (2 Cor. 5:17). Indeed, the very word *regeneration*, or new birth, supposes a new being—not completely or in essence, but with respect to those gracious habits and qualities that the Spirit of God works in the regenerate heart, or what is also called the inward man (2 Cor. 4:16).

Nerimbergius the Jesuit thinks Paul fetched the distinction of inward and outward man from Plato, who also makes such a distinction. Through the work of grace we come to more closely resemble the image of God. Godliness is not a notion or mere fiction but is a supernatural, powerful reality whereby a man has a new nature, for though ungodly he becomes godly. Even as natural things by a physical motion undergo a real transmutation, changing, for example, from cold to hot, so in moral things, the foolish become wise.

Let not people dream of holiness in themselves unless they have been powerfully altered from the state of sin to holiness. This change is compared to a resurrection, and, indeed, regeneration makes no less glorious a change in the soul than it does in the body. As by the latter our vile bodies are made like Christ's glorious body, so our vile and corrupted souls become like His gracious and holy soul. We may truly say that because of supernatural principles we even have the image of God within us, so that it is true what God once did ironically say, "Behold, man is become as one of us" (Gen. 3:22).

Inherent Grace Has Something Internal and Constitutive about It and Flowing from It

Inherent grace works in us as a supernatural permanent principle of holy actions. It has something that is internal and constitutive about it, and something that is consecutive or that flows from it. Godliness is constituted by the nature of the habits of graces (with all their particular differences), just as rationality is that which intrinsically makes a man.

The properties that flow from these are the marks and signs whereby we come to know that grace in us; for as philosophy teaches us, we do not know the forms or internal constitutive differences of things. We only come to know the nature of things by their properties and effects, as the Dutch scholar Joseph Scaliger (1540–1609) said. Hence we have few definitions but many descriptions of things that are derived from their properties and effects. All our knowledge is thus for the most part *a posteriori* (from effect to cause) rather than *a priori* (from cause to effect). A man cannot directly look at the sun because of its glorious luster, but he can behold it indirectly in a basin of water.

Some have argued that we cannot have a demonstrative knowledge of things, moving from cause to effect. To apply this to our purpose, the inward principle and immediate nature of grace is not evident to us but by its effects and proper motions, even as in natural life there is no discerning of life but by its motions. Hence by inherent grace we are said to live (Gal. 2:19–20; Rom. 1:17). So as natural motions are evidence of natural life, supernatural motions are evidence of a supernatural life, with this difference: the latter also requires a peculiar illumination of God's Spirit (Rom. 8).

There Are Different Manifestations of Grace
There are differences among the signs of grace, even as grace itself is distinguished. These include the following:

Gifts of Miracles
Scripture calls the gifts of extraordinary offices, such as that of apostle, *graces*, so that anyone who has an immediate call from God to any duty has a grace from God. However, not all extraordinary prophets have wrought miracles to confirm their doctrine. For example, the apostle John performed no miracles. Yet many times some prophets were furnished with miraculous power. Hence, Christ and His apostles (by virtues derived from Him) wrought diverse miracles, which Galatians 3 says argued for the presence of God's Spirit among them.

Common Graces

There are common graces of God's Spirit that have common effects and signs, such as historical faith, a visible profession, or an outward acceptance of Christ and His laws when there may be no inward change of the heart. For as God calls many by an outward call whom He may not inwardly call, so many who outwardly accept and profess the faith of Christ may not do so inwardly. They have a visible holiness opposing that of the unconverted world (1 Cor. 7:14). They even have a holiness and belief that oppose heathenism and paganism. Hence, in Hebrews 10:29, the apostate who never has had true sanctifying grace is yet said to be sanctified by the blood of Christ. Hence also, those who partake of the outward sacraments are said to be in Christ and to have put on Christ. Upon this ground the apostle writes to the churches as a company of *saints* because of their calling out of the world to have communion and fellowship with Christ.

The notes and marks of common grace are easy and plain to see. A visible number of people may have these so they are accounted as a visible church, and the ordinances are not denied to them, yet they may not have the signs that accompany true salvation. Our intent is not to speak of those notes and characters that are enough to make one a visible member of the church, and so to qualify him as not to deny the ordinances to him. The apostle prays in 1 Corinthians 13:7 that the Corinthians may do no evil that the apostle should have to punish with church censure.

It is true that many Christians satisfy themselves with common characters and signs such as baptism, external profession, and outward abstinence from sin, hence arguing for their sanctification and acceptance with God. We shall speak more on this later. Meanwhile, we must not elevate the signs of grace higher than Scripture does, neither draw them down lower than Scripture does.

Marks of True Faith

The Scripture speaks of marks whereby others may know that we truly belong to God. They are also evidence to our own hearts that we belong to God. For example, John 13:35 says, "By this shall all men know that ye are my disciples, if ye have love one to another." He does not say that if you work miracles or raise the dead you will be His disciples, but "if ye have love one to another." Scripture elsewhere describes what kind of love this ought to be: love not just in word, but also in deed and in truth.

Now, the knowledge we have of other men's graces is always speculative and conjectural, though the apostle expresses himself in a way which suggests that such love is persuasive evidence that saving faith is truly in those who possess it. Though men may give clear and undoubted signs of their wickedness and naughtiness, they cannot give signs of their true godliness and piety because there is nothing in religion that may be expressed to another that cannot flow from a hypocritical heart as well as a sound one. Yet, 1 Corinthians 11 does speak of the end of heresies so that the approved may be made manifest to others. And in 2 Corinthians 3:3, the Corinthians are manifestly declared to be the epistle of Christ. But this is only in respect to a moral certainty so far as men can perceive. Ultimately, it is only God's prerogative to know those who are truly His. Therefore the apostle calls the marks of true belief the "hidden things of the heart."

Scripture describes the signs whereby we may know that *we* are of God and that His Spirit dwells in us. First John 2:3 says we may be sure that we know God if we keep His commandments. John frequently describes the signs of grace in his epistle, as we will see in more detail later. He also says that the knowledge and evidence the godly have of their own grace is far more clear and certain than what they have of one another, insomuch that it is made by some to be a certainty of faith, or at least the sense and experience of faith, to whatever extent such a knowledge is unable to deceive us or be deceived.

Signs of Grace Given Only to the Godly

Whoever has these signs has grace, and he that is without them is without grace. Those with such grace are described in Matthew 13 as being in "good ground." The good and honest heart has a character and constitution that specifically differs from that of hypocrites. Calvin says of reprobates that they are almost affected in like manner as the elect. Yet it is but *almost*, and the difference between them is not general but specific, as is more largely to be showed against the Antinomians on the one side and Arminians on the other. The sorrow and faith of the godly differs significantly from the sorrow and faith of the hypocrite. As the philosophers say, the matter of heavenly bodies is quintessentially different from the sublunary. Thus no extension of parts, intention of degrees, or pretension of time could ever make temporary faith saving faith, for as the maxim in philosophy says, one distinct kind is not compounded of another. But this matter is part of a larger debate.

The Marks of the Godly Vary

Scripture says the marks of a godly man are of different sorts. Some are negative and some positive, but the positive are greater in number than the negative. James 1:27 says pure religion has many positives and one negative, keeping one's self "unspotted from the world." Psalm 15 in its description of a godly man offers six positives and six negatives. Now it is true that neither negatives nor positives, as they are outwardly and visibly expressed, can be a sure testimony of godliness, for a man may do what is good and obtain it from what is evil upon several corrupt grounds, every one of which is like a dead fly in a box of ointment. In Psalm 1 a godly man is described by negatives, first, that he does not sit in the counsel of the wicked, nor does he walk with the ungodly. Yet negative signs do not offer as full a manifestation of grace as positive ones do because grace resides most in the things we ought to do, and good is more good than evil is evil. And our love for the one should be more exercised than our hatred of the other. Therefore, it is deceitful and vain to argue our grace from negatives only, as the Pharisee did in saying, "I am no extorter or adulterer."

On the judgment day, God will proceed according to the good things we have done. And yet most people have no other claim but what they have not done—that they have not been wicked or profane. But godliness does not denote a mere absence of evil. It is a positive concurrence of good.

The Properties and Effects of Grace

The properties and effects of grace may be considered absolutely in terms of properties or relatively in terms of signs. Scripture speaks of both ways. The Scriptures speak in an absolute sense, for example, in Galatians 5:24: "And they that are Christ's have crucified the flesh with the affections and lusts." Also, in 2 Corinthians 5:17: "Therefore if any man be in Christ, he is a new creature: old things are passed away; behold, all things are become new." And finally, in Romans 8:1: "There is therefore now no condemnation to them which are in Christ Jesus, who walk not after the flesh, but after the Spirit."

All such texts are indicative and descriptive of those subjects who are godly in their properties. But John, in his epistles, speaks of these relatively as the signs whereby we may know we are of God. There is a great difference between the two, for a Christian may have all the adjuncts and fruits of grace, yet they are not signs to him because he may be ignorant that they are in him. He may also be strongly persuaded through temptations that he does not have these signs. How often do God's people in sad darkness conclude they are hypocrites, a barren wilderness, or unsavory salt when yet in truth they are the pleasant garden of Christ! If these effects were in them by way of signs, it would be impossible for them to conclude that they were in a state of grace and peace; for a sign is a relative thing, by which we are brought into remembrance of something else. The sacraments are such signs. Rahab's red thread was a sign for the Israelites to remember to preserve her.

Then, too, there are the effects of grace by way of marks and signs, when in the beholding of them we see the causes that wrought them. We see election, justification, adoption, and regeneration from whence they flow, concluding that these great and heavenly things could not be in our soul if Christ and His Spirit were not there. This rich and glorious furniture would not be in our soul, the King of glory would not be there, and the flowers of this garden would not smell so sweet if the wind of God's Spirit did not blow upon them.

Natural vs. Voluntary Marks

Signs can be divided into two groups. First, they are natural if they by necessary consequence signify something else. Thus smoke signifies the presence of a fire. Second, signs are voluntary if they are by will and appointment. The sacraments are voluntary signs, for while there is some natural analogy and fitness in the sacraments between the signs and the things signified, yet the determined appointing of such signification is made by the appointment of God.

Concerning the properties and effects of grace as signs, we cannot say they are merely natural or merely voluntary, for they are of a mixed nature. They are not merely natural, because then whoever has grace working in him would perceive and know he has such grace, even if experience refutes that. Therefore the Spirit's witness and assurance is required in addition to the presence of grace in us. Augustine rightly said that whoever truly believes perceives in himself that he does believe. This saying is much celebrated and used against Roman Catholic doubting. As our divines say, as he that has fire in his bosom has been sealed by fire, and he that tastes a sweet object perceives the sweetness of it, and he that is awake knows that he is awake, so he that has the operations of God's Spirit within him knows these are wrought by God, and he is not deceived.

But while this is true of the genuine and proper work of supernatural life in us, yet there may be several impediments to this assurance due to sin, especially inward unbelief and sin or outward obstructions, such as God's deserting and forsaking of us so that we cannot perceive the good things He has done for us. Thus they are not signs in a mere natural way. Nor can we say they are merely voluntary signs, for the effects of grace are the proper and genuine fruits of grace, and he who has sanctification also necessarily has justification. These are therefore evidences of our interest in Christ, yet they are manifested only by the light of the Spirit. As some philosophers say, the stars have an innate light of their own, but they are not conspicuous and visible without the light of the sun. Likewise the gracious fruit of supernatural principles in us have an aptitude and fitness to make us know that we are in Christ, but they cannot remove all darkness without the Spirit of God, even as only the light of the sun, not of the stars, can dispel the darkness of the night.

The Importance of Faith

We should not so gaze upon ourselves to find graces in our hearts that we forget those acts of faith whereby we immediately close with Christ and rely upon Him only for our justification. The fear of doing this has made some deny the validity of using signs as evidence of our justification. And indeed it is true that many of God's children, while they are studying and examining themselves to see whether grace is in their souls (and that upon the discovery of graces, are persuaded of their justification), may very much neglect those choice and principal acts of faith whereby they may have acquiescency and recumbency upon Christ for acceptation with God. This is as if old Jacob rejoiced so much about the chariot Joseph sent, whereby he knew that his son was alive, that he failed to desire to see Joseph himself. Thus while you are so full of joy about perceiving grace in your soul, you forget to joy in Christ Himself, who is more excellent than all your graces. We will consider this in more depth later.

All the Signs Are Not Necessary for Assurance of Salvation

The Scripture attributes blessedness and salvation to several of its signs. Sometimes the fear of God is a sign, sometimes a poverty of spirit, sometimes hungering and thirsting after righteousness, sometimes repentance, sometimes love, and sometimes patience. If a godly man can find any of these signs in himself he may be assured of his salvation and justification, even though he does not see all the signs in himself. Many people of God perceive one sign in themselves when they cannot see another. So it is not the number of signs that determines our justification.

The learned speak about the marks and signs of Christ and the Antichrist. It may happen that individuals will have some of the signs that belong to the

Messiah, but not all (for only He who is truly Christ has them all). Likewise, there are many descriptions of Antichrist, and in time others besides him may have some of those marks that identify the spirit of Antichrist but none have them all cumulatively and collectively as the true Antichrist. It is not so with the marks of grace, for if a believer upon good grounds can be persuaded of having but one mark, he may undoubtedly conclude that he has all the marks, even though he does not yet feel them in himself.

The Signs and Marks of Grace Are to Be Used

Scripture says the marks of true grace are to be insisted upon and used. Hypocrites may be strongly confident that they have the marks, when indeed they do not have them. It is therefore no argument against the signs of grace that a hypocrite is confident he has them, and yet is deceived. The wise virgins who had prepared enough oil knew their bridegroom and went out in confidence to meet him. The foolish virgins who lacked enough oil also went out with confidence to meet the bridegroom.

Do not despair of discerning the true marks of grace in yourself because others have falsely persuaded themselves of such marks. Many a dreamer has pleased himself that he enjoyed riches or delicacies, yet it was only in a dream. However, the man who is awake knows when he has riches and is not deceived. A hypocrite may be bold because he feels secure in God's favor and may

die with confidence, calling God his God and Christ his
Christ. But this does not hinder the true believer from
knowing he is in the right and is not deceived. In matters
of religion, the Turk is confident of his doctrine and the
Jew of his and the Roman Catholic of his, yet it does not
follow that the Protestant therefore may not confidently
know he has the truth, and all others are deceived.

The Signs of Grace Will Be Consistent
with Their Nature

If the essence of a thing is imperfect, the marks of it
will also be imperfect. This is a rule of great comfort
in practice, for the godly look for perfect signs of grace
in themselves. If they find hypocrisy, carnal ends, lukewarmness, or any such faults, they often begin to doubt
their entire state. But they should consider that just as
their graces are imperfect, neither can the signs of them
be perfect. Hence though we grant that godly men such
as Hezekiah and Paul were comforted by the truth of
grace in themselves, yet this was not due to any merit or
cause in them for justification, for they also discovered
much imperfection in themselves.

CHAPTER 9

Using Signs for Assurance and Proving That They Evidence Justification

We have laid down several propositions leading to a clearer discovery of the truth about signs or marks of grace. Now we will show the lawfulness and duty of both ministers and people to proceed by this method. For though my proper work is to speak only of the fruits of grace as they evidence sanctification within a believer, yet I shall also examine how we may prove our justification by inherent gracious qualifications within us.

This is often expressly written and preached against, for by this means godly Christians are often plunged into several entanglements of conscience and know not how to resolve them. I shall, therefore, God helping me, present arguments to confirm this duty. However, let us first identify what is the true practical case and answer some questions related to this.

Questions about Assurance

1. Should a Christian in his first act of faith, by which he closes with Christ, applies Him, and is engrafted into Him, see inherent qualifications in himself by way of signs and evidences?

That is not possible, for we must first be implanted into Christ by faith before there can be any fruits demonstrating our being in Him. In 1 John 2:5, the apostle John observes that obedience to God's commandments is a sign that we are in Christ; therefore, we are in Christ prior to this by faith. Thus in all the promises offered to a Christian, who is loaded with sin, inviting him to come to Christ, that does not require knowing with certainty what condition he is in, whether his grace be true or not, but only that he has the sense and feeling of his own unworthiness in apprehending Christ.

It is therefore wrong to preach that you may not rely upon Christ for justification until you have the certainty and evidence in your heart whether grace is truly in you or not. Scripture says blessed are those who mourn and who hunger and thirst for righteousness (Matt. 5:4, 6); and calls to those who are burdened that they will have relief, even though they may not have certainty of God's work of grace in them at that time. We must diligently maintain this truth because upon this rock many a tender Christian may split himself.

2. Should a godly man in sad temptations, having no light at all, make search at that time for the motions and workings of grace in his soul?

The answer is no, for such a search would breed further fears and uncertainties. The soul in such temptation is like muddied water in which nothing is clearly represented. As during the night one's imagination is prone to see nothing but objects of fear and terror, so is the heart in the midst of such desolations prone to fear. When he is in such a state, David calls upon his soul to trust in God and to wait on Him as the only remedy. Indeed, in such cases the proper duty of a godly man is to throw himself boldly upon the promises of God, as did Peter when he ventured to walk upon water after Christ called him to do so. Because of the promises and gracious invitations of God, we go to Him relying upon His goodness. As Job said, "Though he slay me, yet will I trust in him" (Job 13:15).

3. Should a godly man look for signs such as will fully rise up to the obligation and perfection of the law?

Again, no, for it is plain that such signs cannot be found. It is therefore an odious mistake for an antinomian to argue against universal obedience as a sign, because no man can perform such. Even if this obedience is limited to a heart's purpose, no one has a constant purpose because of the many corrupt suggestions and lusts that plague his heart. No one should promote such signs, for, since no one is perfect, so no one should look for perfection. Instead, the least grace discovered in the soul that is sincere and upright, though not enough to satisfy the desire of a Christian, ought to be enough to confirm him of his interest in Christ.

4. May the inherent qualifications of grace be evidences without the luster of God's Spirit?

No, for all theologians agree that this certainty arises efficaciously from the Spirit of God; therefore, as Ephesians 1 says, sealing is attributed to the Spirit of God. We must not oppose a godly life or attribute graces only to the Spirit of God, but conjoin them, even as the certainty we have about the Scripture is based not only upon those arguments that prove the divinity of the Scripture by noting such attributes as the style, majesty, or purity of the Spirit of God, but also because God's Spirit persuades us of such. So it is here, that God's Spirit seals our interest in Christ by the graces which are wrought in us.

5. Should the work of God's Spirit in us be rested upon as the cause or merit of our justification?

No, this is a pharisaical Roman Catholic idea that should be detested. A Christian who finds such graces in himself should not base the comfort of his justification upon them or rest on them instead of Christ. Rather, he should consider these as signs of Christ's dwelling in him and so rejoice in God's love and be thankful to God.

6. Is the work of God's Spirit in us through sanctification the only witness to our salvation, or is there also an immediate testimony of God's Spirit to the soul apart from the gracious fruits of holiness?

I believe the fruits of holiness are the only safe and sure witness of sanctification, which, for the most part, Scripture commends.[1] This being premised, I offer the following arguments to support the idea that assurance of justification and regeneration issues from the fruits of holiness.

Argument 1: See how true grace differs from counterfeit grace. Scripture offers descriptions of the characteristics of true grace and false. Those differences are diligently

---

1. Burgess and several other Puritans were concerned that if they maintained that the immediate testimony of the Spirit would be embraced as a distinct form of assurance it would promote practical antinomianism and tend to exalt experience for its own sake. Consequently, Burgess interpreted the Westminster Confession of Faith (18.2) to be saying that assurance from the testimony of the Spirit and from inward evidences of grace are one and the same. Other Puritans, such as William Twisse and Thomas Goodwin, believed that the Westminster Assembly intended the direct testimony of the Spirit through the Word to be a distinct form of assurance. For a more nuanced discussion of this difference among the Puritans, see Joel R. Beeke, *The Quest for Full Assurance of Faith: The Legacy of Calvin and His Successors* (Edinburgh: Banner of Truth, 1999), 142–46.

pressed so that every man may take heed and discern one from the other. For example, in Matthew 13, our Savior in the parable of the sower describes with precision the differences in the soils upon which the seed is flung—that is, the various ways men's hearts are affected by the preaching of the Word. Some hearts receive the Word far more readily than others, yet only the good and honest heart truly accepts the Word and is changed by it. Thus our Savior says, "He that hath ears to hear, let him hear."

This matter deeply concerns us, for in this parable our Lord tells us to examine ourselves to see how the Word of God has prevailed in us. If those who listen to Christ cannot tell whether they are good ground or thorny, such descriptions would have no purpose. Likewise in John 10:4–5, Christ describes His sheep as those who hear His voice and follow Him. They will not heed a stranger's voice and follow him; rather, they will flee from the stranger.

It is good to observe that, as in other places of Scripture, one mark of grace is to take heed of sin and to love holiness. So here, it is made a sign of Christ's sheep that they take heed of errors and false teachers and are afraid of false doctrines and wicked ways. Oh how necessary it is to press this sign of grace in these times! How afraid you should be of being led aside from the true faith by people with deceitful pretexts. Colossians 3:12 offers a catalog of graces that flow from election such as kindness, humility, gentleness, and patience. Other passages in Scripture that describe the properties of godliness urge us to see whether we express them in our lives or not.

Argument 2: We are commanded in Scripture to make this search, whether or not grace be truly in us. If such an effort were not lawful and useful, why would the Holy Spirit prescribe it? How clear 1 Corinthians 13:5 is in telling us to examine and prove ourselves to see whether we are in the faith. If anyone should argue against the apostle that this cannot be done, or that it is derogatory to Christ, or that it prompts us to rest in ourselves, let him also consider Galatians 6:4, which urges every man to search for and examine his works. We are also to consider the nature, grounds, and intentions of these works. This is commended because of its profitable effects, for thereby a person shall rejoice only in himself rather than by comparing himself to others who may be worse or because he is considered godly in the judgment of others. His comfort will be from within.

Observe how rejoicing in oneself is lawful when it is accompanied by a thankful acknowledgment of God's grace bestowed on one's soul. However, in the matter of justification, any rejoicing or boasting in oneself is excluded. First Peter 1:10 makes this clear. It urges believers to give all diligence to make their calling and election sure. Such election cannot be made surer with respect to God or itself, but only in respect to us, that we may be more persuaded of it. How does this work? The apostle shows us in the verses preceding: by adding grace to grace, and causing those things to abound in us. Thus finding assurance by way of signs and marks is plainly taught by Scripture.

Argument 3: Consider those places in Scripture where the godly took their graces as signs and testimonies of God's love. They thereby received much comfort, even using these signs of grace as an argument for mercy in their prayers—not by way of merit or causality, but as the effect of God's grace and as the basis for asking God to perfect His own work.

Second Kings 20:3 tells us how King Hezekiah labored more diligently than any king before him to rid Israel of idols. Yet this king, being the true Hercules who purged the Augean stable, was struck with a mortal disease from God. In what exigencies was he then plagued! A great army was against him, he had no visible successors to his throne, all of his reforms were in danger of reversing themselves, and his own death was imminent. See then how he comes to God, pleading upon his own graces by saying, "Remember now how I have walked before thee in truth and with a perfect heart" (v. 3). Likewise Nehemiah pleaded, "Remember me, O my God...and wipe not out my good deeds that I have done for the house of my God" (Neh. 13:14).

Such cries are not indicative of Roman Catholic theology, as if Hezekiah or Nehemiah thought their good deeds were perfect and thus a cause for mercy, for Nehemiah says in verse 22: "Remember me, O my God, and spare me according to the greatness of *thy* mercy." His good deeds were ineffective without God's mercy and pardon. They also fell far short of perfection or merit.

Yet these examples do confirm the truth that a godly man may take comfort from his graces as signs and testimonies of God's love to him. And this plea for God's help based upon personal piety is not peculiar to the Old Testament. In the New Testament, the apostle Paul, who was a continual trumpet of God's grace, counted all his righteousness as dung and dross before Christ. Yet he too proceeded by way of signs, for in 2 Timothy 4:7–8 Paul says, "I have fought a good fight, I have finished my course…henceforth there is laid up for me a crown of righteousness." And in 2 Corinthians 1:12, Paul says that our rejoicing lies in this: the testimony of our conscience, that we have conducted ourselves with godly sincerity in the world. So in these words of Paul we see how a Christian may exalt Christ and His grace and discount his own righteousness for justification while, at the same time, taking comfort in his righteousness manifested in sanctification.

The history of Job also confirms this truth, for though Job's friends believed that God had cast him off as a hypocrite, yet Job would not part with the comfort of his integrity till death. Job had no immediate consolations from God, for the arrows of the Almighty had stuck deep into him and there was nothing to comfort him but his upright heart. Likewise, the godly man's sense and feeling of God's grace within him is a great bulwark in a time of temptation.

Roman Catholic theology cannot weaken this truth with the assertion that the experimental affections felt in religious duties only beget a conjectural knowledge, not assurance of faith, since the object thereof is not revealed in Scripture. It may well be granted that this sense of believing is not an act of faith, and a man does not properly believe that he believes but only inwardly perceives and feels that he believes. Yet this sense is not fallacious, for it proceeds from a supernatural principle within.

Argument 4: Scripture speaks of grace as fruit. We see this in passages like Luke 3:8, Galatians 5:22, and 2 Corinthians 9:10. Our Savior lays down an undeniable maxim in Matthew 12:33 that just as a good tree is known by its good fruit, a good heart is also a treasury from which good things flow. Though some trees without reason and sense cannot be known by their fruit, most can be. Likewise, the children of God by their good fruit are known to both themselves and others. Yes, they are more known to themselves than others because no man knows the things of a man save the spirit of a man. Thus the grace that is evident in the workings thereof is often compared to life (see Gal. 2:22). Now as a natural life is discerned by its actions, as by so many signs, so also is supernatural life. However, as in some diseases the affected party does not perceive any life, neither do the godly always perceive their spiritual life during some sad temptations.

Argument 5: There are many promises in Scripture that speak comfort and encouragement to those who have various exercises of grace. These promises would afford no comfort at all if a Christian could not by way of signs know that he had them. In several places Scripture attributes blessedness to the man who fears God, keeps His law, is undefiled, endures persecution for a good cause, and is pure and meek in spirit. What encouragement could a godly man have without this practical syllogism?

+ *Major premise*: Scripture says the man who fears God is blessed.

+ *Minor premise*: I fear God.

+ *Conclusion*: Therefore, I am blessed.

Though the majority of this proposition is based on Scripture, yet the assumption itself is based on experience, for a godly man who fears God is persuaded to do so by the Holy Spirit. Therefore, the conclusion is undeniable.

Argument 6: Many places in Scripture support this truth. The First Epistle of John expresses itself most comprehensively this way, as if John is purposely determined to destroy any other view. In 1 John 2:3–5, for example, John says we may know that we know God if we keep His commandments. The apostle compares our imperfect or hypocritical knowledge with the true knowledge of Christ. True knowledge is operative and brings obedience, whereas what the hypocrites know affords only light without heat.

The apostle lays down two propositions: First, that he who has true knowledge of Christ will observe His commandments and, second, that we may see by his observation of God's law his knowledge is good. He speaks to the same purpose in the following two verses: first, because our faith must not only be carried to Christ who is our propitiation for sin, but also to Him as an example whom we are called to imitate, for we are to walk as Christ walked. By this imitation of Christ, we may know we are in Christ when we observe two things: First, that by faith we have been implanted in Christ and, second, that we discover our being in Him by our holy walk. We do not plead for sanctification as evidence of justification in the sense that our graces put us into Christ and justify us, but only that these are testimonies and witnesses of the truth of our truly being in Christ.

First John 3:10 says the children of God and the children of the devil are manifest in that he who is born of God sins not, meaning that he does not sin out of such a full and habitual purpose of will that his sin extinguishes the seed of grace within him. The manifestation of the children of God or of the devil is conjectural to others, yet the godly man, whose heart is cured by regeneration of the innate guile which cleaves to it, is also comforted that he is clear of deceit.

In verse 13, the apostle exhorts the godly not to wonder if the world hates them. To amplify their consolation he says in verse 14 that we may know that we are translated from death to life if we love others who believe. It is a great sign of godliness to love another person because he is godly, and the more he is godly, the more we love him. On the other hand, to hate another because his ways are good and yours are evil—which is all too common—demonstrates that you are of the devil. Now, this love of our brothers does not *cause* our translation from death to life. The very word *translated* supposes it a grace of God from outside of us, while the love itself is only a sign.

Because a Roman Catholic and a Jew love their own, they may often think they are godlier than others when in truth they are deceived. But a true godly man is not hindered from loving another who is godly and having solid comfort therein. We will discuss this in more detail later.

Having identified love of fellow believers as a sign, the apostle says that this is not a feigned love, but a real and operative love, for love is like fire—if it is not active we can argue that it does not exist at all. So the apostle, as is peculiar to him, uses this again as a sign so that by this we may know that we are of the truth and be assured (as the Greek implies) that even if our heart is full of doubts and unbelief, the discovery of such graces within us is enough to satisfy us that we belong to God, providing our hearts do not condemn us and we have confidence toward God.

Now here are two doubts: first, he whose heart does not condemn him of much pride, vanity, neglect, and other sins cannot have confidence. The apostle speaks of such condemning for total and reigning hypocrisy, however, and not for the partial corruption which is in even the godliest. A second doubt may be of those who persecute the truth and the people of God, as the Jews and Saul of Tarsus did. Their hearts did not condemn them for what they did, but rather they thought they did God good service thereby. But the apostle speaks of Christians who are endued with the true doctrine of the knowledge of Christ out of His Word. Those whose hearts reprove them not for hypocrisy may have boldness with God. Thus the apostle frequently urges the fruits of godliness by way of signs, but these may suffice to confirm the doctrine.

Argument 7: Our fruits may prove that we are justified and sanctified. If a Christian could not prove the graces of justification and sanctification by its fruits, it would be impossible for him to know when such graces are in him. This is what the Roman Catholics say. But this is false, first, because though a man's heart is naturally deceitful, yet when it is regenerated, God takes away its guile and transforms it into a heart that is sincere and cannot lie.

Second, if we have assurance by God's Spirit, one may question why we need evidences of inherent graces, saying that may be as useless as lighting a candle when the sun is shining. Yet both are necessary, for the testimony of the Spirit and the evidence of graces make up one complete witness. They are therefore not to be disjoined, much less opposed to each other.

Third, it may be thought prejudicial in two ways, either to Christ or His righteousness, as if the comfort from inherent graces takes us away from relying wholly upon Christ. We have already explained how the apostle Paul, who exalted Christ and His righteousness, yet took comfort from the graces wrought in himself. It may be thought that the discovery of grace in us may make us proud and secure; but this does not necessarily follow, because with such graces the gracious heart is stirred up to more thankfulness, watchfulness, and fruitfulness, lest we lose such a treasure.

Practical Conclusions

Let us thus try ourselves by the marks and signs that Scripture gives us, for certainly there was never a time in which those marks of grace have been more necessary than now. How many place religion in opinions, in disputations, and in revelations! Yet the true power of godliness and mortification was so neglected that the apostle James in his epistle and Paul constantly spoke against the Gnostics and other sects that tried to make a religion of knowledge and to arrogate that only to themselves. Thus the apostles pressed the necessity of a godly and holy life.

Therefore, that you may not deceive yourself, study the Scripture and the characters of grace, for they may teach you those signs by which you may comfort yourself. Personal duties, great enlargements, and maintaining a specific church government are not true marks of holiness, considering what Christ says about the properties of His sheep, which are not to listen to strangers and to flee from errors. Certainly our Savior in describing the branches that are in Him took no notice of their leaves or their blossoms, but only of their fruit.

Be afraid lest Christ's coming to you be like His coming to the fig tree, only to see leaves on its branches but no fruit, whereupon He pronounced the curse, "Never may fruit grow on thee anymore." So Christ may find many opinions, disputations, abilities, and outward duties in you who claim to profess God, but not true holiness. Therefore He may curse you, saying, "Never may fruit grow on you. You produce leaves and branches, but never produce fruit." It is fearful to think of many who live with such a curse upon them, for holiness of life must be joined to the abilities of the mind. As it is said, good and holy actions adorn you more than rings of gold and silver upon your hands.

CHAPTER 10

The Lawfulness and Obligation of Proceeding by Signs, and Answering Doubts

Additional Scriptures prove the lawfulness and obligation of proceeding by way of signs, but because there are different expositions of them I shall rank these in order of debated texts, which probably at least confirm this truth.

1. *Romans* 8:16. This verse says, "The Spirit itself beareth witness with our spirit, that we are the sons of God." In these words we may observe the author of the testimony, the manner, and the object of it. The author is said to be the Spirit Himself. The apostle says it is no presumption or arrogance for the people of God to call God Father, because they are encouraged and emboldened to do so by the Spirit of God. It is not a delusion from the devil, but an assurance from God's Spirit.

In the next place, the manner of testimony is a conjoined testimony, not a single one. The Spirit bears witness with our spirit. It is true that Hugo Grotius (1583–1645), a scholarly jurist in the Dutch Republic, takes the word, though compounded, for a simple one, citing 2 Corinthians 1:12 and 5:11 where the apostle speaks of the conscience bearing witness. But these texts are not cogent to this argument, for the conscience in testifying does witness with another, which is God, and therefore the witness of the conscience is not a single testimony. It must therefore be understood as a joint witness.

Still, the question remains: Who is the partner joined with God's Spirit in this action? Some think the spirit of a man cannot be the cowitness, but only the subject that receives the testimony. They thus render the text, "The Spirit beareth witness *to* our spirit," not *with* our spirit. Others say this joint witness is Christ, for in verse 10 the apostle assures us that Christ dwells in us. Then, as His Spirit makes us cry, "Abba, Father," so the Spirit with Christ and the Father are thought to be the same as what 1 John 5:7 says, "There are three that bear record in heaven."

Still others understand that voice produced in us by God's Spirit to be the gift of regeneration. This is how Chrysostom understands it. In this sense both witnesses will be one, whether we translate it *to* or *with* our spirit. So then the meaning is that the Spirit of God bears witness to us with those gifts and graces that are the fruit of the Spirit. Thus the apostle speaks not of such an immediate testimony as the prophets had in their visions when they heard God speak immediately to them, but by and with our spirits which are enlightened and sanctified, so that though the Spirit of God is the only author of this assurance, yet it is in an ordinary way made evident by the fruits of the Spirit.

The Spirit of God may be seen as witnessing this infallibly and surely, or else conjecturally and by way of probability. Roman Catholic commentators say it is the latter way, but it is very unworthy and derogatory to make the Spirit of God author only of a conjectural certainty, for a divine testimony cannot be anything less than infallible. Certainly if the apostle said of the conscience, which has much error and falsehood in it, that it has a thousand witnesses, how much more may this be said of the Spirit of God? We shall speak more on this later.

2. *Ephesians 1:13.* This verse says, "In whom also after that ye believed, ye were sealed with that holy Spirit of promise." Witnessing or assurance is metaphorically expressed here by sealing, which means to ratify and confirm things. It says that God seals us not for His sake, but ours, that we may be persuaded of His love. God does not seal as a merchant surveys his wares that he may know them, but as a father testifies or offers deeds or gifts to assure his children of his favor toward them.

But you may ask, What is this sealing? The metaphor declares that as a seal makes an impression of its likeness in wax, so God in sealing makes an impression of His own holy image upon us. This assures us that we are His. Those who understand this sealing as the extraordinary and miraculous gifts of God's Spirit do not hit the mark because these are not necessary signs of adoption. Also, they are not bestowed upon every particular believer.

We must therefore view sealing as one of the sanctifying graces of God's Spirit. The faith whereby we first receive Christ is not the evidence of such graces (as some plead) because it is after our believing, for the word is in the past tense.[1] That it refers to holiness does also appear in the words "sealed with that Holy Spirit of promise." The Spirit of God is called the Spirit of the promise. He is called holy because of the holiness He works in His children, which is their sealing. Thus, as God the Father is said to seal Christ when He gave Him those abilities that were required of a mediator, anointing Him with all graces and witnessing by miracles that Jesus was God's Son, thus does God the Father also seal His children by furnishing them with all the graces of His Holy Spirit, for by these they know they are of God.

---

1. Following Calvin, John Owen disagrees with Burgess's stress here on the seal coming after believing, but believes that Ephesians 1:13 could better be translated as "upon believing"—that is, that the Spirit's sealing transpires in the moment of regeneration. Other Puritans, such as Richard Sibbes, speak of both an objective sealing in the moment of regeneration and a subjective sealing that grows together with the believer's degree of assurance. Cf. Beeke, *Quest for Full Assurance*, 201–8.

3. *1 John 5:8.* The third text says, "There are three that bear witness on earth: water, and blood, and the Spirit." I would quickly tire you out if I commented on all that has been said by expositors on this text. So, I shall instead briefly assert the one exposition that is most suitable to other places of Scripture.

By *water,* the text refers to what purifies and cleanses us from the filth of sin. We receive this through Christ outwardly in what is called the seal of baptism. By *blood,* the text refers to the forgiveness of the guilt of sin, which satisfies God's wrath. This is sealed to us in the sacrament of the Lord's Supper. The *Spirit* in the text refers to God's Spirit, which does not immediately testify to us for He is a witness in heaven. Rather, the Spirit testifies by the fruits of grace, stirring up faith in us to a vigorous and powerful way of holiness, by which we perceive the fruit of water and blood accomplished in our souls. I will not stay much longer on various explanations of these texts; however, I will propound some objections to make the duty of going by signs clearer and easier for you.

Objection 1: Does it not argue weakness and unbelief in a Christian to walk by signs? Does this not denigrate the glorious promise of grace, as if it were not enough?

Answer 1. Signs do not argue for absolute weakness, but comparative weakness only. In heaven, all sacraments, which are signs and seals, shall cease. Whether

Adam had any sacraments while in the state of perfection is disputed. Some say the Tree of Life was one, but it could not be a sacrament in that particular sense as ours are in sealing the remission of sin and mortification of it, but in a more general way. For the sacraments do two things: first, they in general confirm God as our God and us as His children, and also confirm our communion with others. In this sense Christ was baptized and thus made partaker of other sacraments (for we may not say Christ therefore used the sacraments in order to sanctify them, because they were sanctified by their institution). Second, the sacraments signify what is special in them, such as the remission of sins and increase of grace. Thus, only the members of the militant church may partake of them.

Answer 2. It cannot be denied that it is a nobler and more excellent way to believe in the promise by a faith of dependency and adherence than to believe based upon the sense and evidences of graces in us. Yet this latter is lawful and encouraged by God. For this is why God gave the gift of miracles to some, that by such wonderful things appearing to sense, they might be persuaded to believe in God. A clear example of this is Thomas in John 20:24–29, who was initially reproved for his unbelief—but then, upon seeing and feeling the wounds of Christ, makes the clear confession, "My Lord and my God" (v. 28). This faith was laudable in him, but yet our

Savior says, "Blessed are they that have not seen and yet have believed" (v. 29).

Though Thomas is not excluded from blessedness (for he did believe by seeing), yet those who believe without signs show a more blessed work of grace upon themselves. We may therefore believe because of God's Word, and we may believe because of our senses, which may be a help to our faith. God has appointed sacraments for this end. Not that the things we see are properly the object of our faith, for faith is the evidence of things not seen (Heb. 11:1). Thus Thomas had faith based upon the object of his sight and feeling, which was the wounds of Christ's body, as well as faith based upon the object of his faith, which was Jesus Christ as God.

Thus in the sacraments, the object of our senses is not the object of our faith. We are only helped by our senses, which serve as motives to believe. Although the need to be helped by the senses to believe is a comparative weakness, yet because of the condition we are in it is also a duty to be encouraged. Hence he that believed because of miracles did his duty and did not sin in doing so. Yes, Ahaz was severely rebuked because he would not accept a sign to confirm his faith in the promise that God had made for the kingdom's deliverance.

Objection 2: When we receive evidence from our graces, do we not receive a human testimony as a witness of the things of God? Is that not incongruous? Since we are the

children of God the witness ought to be divine, not human.
Consequently, we should reject evidences of faith by our
sanctification.

Answer 1. A human testimony may first be necessary to believe what is divine. In this sense, there is a
human witness to the things of God. Thus the woman
of Samaria testified of Christ, and those who heard her
were moved by her testimony, although they believed
afterward because of Christ Himself. Thus also John the
Baptist bore witness of Christ. In this sense our divines
acknowledge the church's authority along with Augustine, who said he would not have believed the Scriptures
had not the authority of the church moved him.

Answer 2. We do not say that the graces of God's
Spirit can or do witness by themselves, for the sealing
and witnessing are efficiently from the Spirit of God
and are only the means by which God's Spirit makes
Himself known. As colors cannot be seen on an object
without light shining upon them, so neither can we
behold the good things God has wrought for us without
the aid of the Spirit of God.

Answer 3. The graces of God are not human testimonies, but divine and infallible. Their testimony
is supernatural, both in the efficient cause and in the
means by which they act. Thus the godly actions in us
are not of human origin or done by the power of free
will, but are divine and arise from the supernatural
principle of grace within us. Thus neither should this

testimony or consolation flowing from it be attributed to our reason and understanding, but unto God alone.

Roman Catholic teaching regards these experimental works of grace within us to provide only moral conjectures and probable indications of God's Spirit dwelling in us, only they say that these works may provide such a certainty that they may morally exclude all doubting. As an example, Roman Catholics say we may be as sure that we are in the state of grace as that there is a city of Rome or Constantinople, even if we have not seen those places. This is not enough, however, because Roman Catholics deny that these signs are the infallible witness of God's Spirit.

Objection 3: Aren't evidences of grace by signs useless, seeing that the Spirit of God immediately works in our hearts a strong assurance of faith? And having this assurance, what need have we of anything else? If we have the sun, what need have we of a candle?

Hence some have reduced the whole doctrine of evidences to two heads: First, the immediate revelation made by God's Spirit to the soul. This is like the sunbeams which dart into a dark room. The second is the soul that receives evidence by faith. It has been formerly taught that faith is the full persuasion of God's love to a man's self. If this is so, the whole business of evidence seems to be accomplished before we come to any signs.

Answer 1. To answer this objection, we must look for Scriptures which prove that God's Spirit has spoken clearly to a man by an immediate testimony that his sins are forgiven and he is therefore in the state of grace. Although we take for granted that God immediately comes into the soul and witnesses to it, yet we have seen by the texts we have already cited that it is more in harmony with Scripture to make its testimony active with respect to the effects and fruits thereof. Some divines do not deny the possibility of God's immediate testimony, but they conclude that the ordinary and safe way is to look for the testimony which is evident in the effects and fruits of God's Spirit. Therefore when we speak of the Spirit of God's revelation, which is often mentioned in Scripture, we may either conceive of it as revealed by an immediate influence, or else that the Spirit of God enlightens the understanding to see the grounds and reasons why it should thus be persuaded.

There is a vast difference between these two, however, for Scripture says a believer is fully persuaded of the divine authority of the Scripture through the Spirit of God's revelation of this to him. This may be understood two ways, either by immediate dictates of the Spirit, telling the soul it is so, or else by enlightening the understanding to see those implanted arguments that persuade him of Scripture's authority.

As it is thus for the Word, so it is for the work of God's Spirit in us, for we come to be persuaded of God's love to us and assured of it not because of an authority testifying this to us immediately, but because God's Spirit so efficiently enlightens the heart that we see His gracious operations and are confidently persuaded of God's love to us. Thus the sun manifests itself to be the sun by the light that comes from it. A learned man proves himself to be learned by the information he discovers, and the Spirit of God with His holy operations manifests Himself to be the Spirit of God dwelling in us. But this we shall speak more about later.

Answer 2. Faith is not full persuasion. The scriptural terms that express faith speak of it as an affiance (i.e., a pledge) and adherence rather than a persuasion, for it is a reflex act in the soul whereby we know that we know (as the apostle John expresses it) and that we do truly repent and believe.

Answer 3. Even if such evidences were granted, still the evidence by way of signs would not be in vain, for it has pleased God to multiply those things which may confirm our faith. Thus, though every word of God has immutable variety in it, yet it is also confirmed with an oath for the sake of men, to end all those controversies which diffidence and distrust may raise between God and us. The apostle also says in Hebrews 6:18 "that by two immutable things, in which it was impossible for God to lie, we might have a strong consolation." And again, although God's promises to us will not be broken, and nothing can be surer than that, yet He adds sacraments to seal and confirm His promises to us. Therefore, even if such assurances were granted, yet there is also great usefulness in the evidences we have by signs.

Objection 4: A universal maxim states that no one may be at the same time both the person questioned and the judge. But this absurdity would follow if we proceeded by evidences, for the heart of a man is questioned as to whether it has true graces in it or not, and the heart must also be judge of this at the same time.

We answer that this does not necessarily follow, for though the heart be in supposed guilt and so questioned, yet the judging of this is by the Spirit of God, and our hearts are not actually guilty but sanctified; all this is according to the rules of Scripture. But indeed the absurdity does follow in a pharisaical or formal man who is altogether carnal and has not the Spirit of God or any supernatural principles; for when he acquits himself, he is both the guilty person and the judge as well. By this means he gives false judgment, calling evil good and darkness light, but it is not so with believers.

Objection 5: It is difficult, if not impossible, to have certainty by means of signs. For any sign, such as love of the brethren, must first be explained as the love that exists because people are brothers and have the kind of love that proceeds from upright principles, pure motives, and many other qualifications, which are as hard to know as the inward root of grace itself.

Answer 1. First, Scripture gives many signs and symptoms of grace, so if a man cannot find all of them in himself, yet discovers some—even only one—he may conclude that all the rest are there. This is because the harmony and connection of grace is compared to the image of God, which consists of all its due lineaments. Thus it is wrong for a Christian who can find little of God's Spirit in him to doubt that he has nothing at all.

Answer 2. There is a twofold knowledge. One is distinct and demonstrative; it is *a priori,* from the cause to the effect. With this we know the principles and root of grace within us and may thus proceed to the effects of it. The other is more general and proceeds from the effects to the cause, or *a posteriori.* With this we proceed from the streams to the fountain. This kind of knowledge is the easiest to grasp. We are also most prone to think in terms of effects to cause. The Spirit of God generally guides us in this way since it is most suitable to our natures.

Answer 3. Though a man may doubt some signs, it does not follow that he will doubt all of them because he may be tempted to favor one sign more than another and perceive one sign more easily than another. So a godly man may argue from what is less known to what is more known. Even with respect to the canon of Scripture, some have doubted whether some books are canonical because the arguments of divine authority are clearer in other books than in them. Yet in those books concerning the authority of which they were not tempted, they were at last induced to believe the authority of those that were controversial. That may also be true of the signs of grace. It is more difficult to find some of them in ourselves than others, yet we may proceed from those that are easier to see to those that are more difficult.

Objection 6: A man may be easily deceived in the ways of signs, which may be seen in this practical syllogism:

- *Everyone who loves the brethren is translated from death to life.*

- *I love the brethren.*

- *Therefore, I am translated from death to life.*

Answer: In his *Treatise of Justification*, Cornwell denies that the faith wrought in such a practical syllogism is attributable to the power of the Lord Almighty.[2] He says it is only the result of human reason and is therefore only human faith. This is a very dangerous assertion. It is comparable to what the Jesuits would like to impose upon the Protestants concerning a doctrinal faith, saying that that is only a formula for getting at the

---

2. Burgess refers to Francis Cornwell, *A Conference Mr. John Cotton Held at Boston with the Elders of New England* (London: J. Dawson, 1646), 17.

truth, by which the Jesuits would conclude the Protestants have no faith because the object of faith must be, according to the Protestants, the mere Word of God. They say there is nothing that the Protestants believe that was not concluded by way of a syllogism, and in this syllogism, the assumption is not to be found in Scripture. Or they say the Protestants err in making the inference, so they have no true conclusion.

But all this is sophistry, for just as a near and immediate conclusion is in the principle, so it is believed with the same faith that the principle is believed, and when a man by reason makes a conclusion, his reason is only the instrument, not the argument, of his faith. His reason is not the ground of his faith, nor does it suggest the matter to be believed, but is the instrument he uses to discover it. As he that digs in a mine of gold uses the same instruments in removing the earth as in covering it, he does not make gold but only discovers it.

As for this practical syllogism, it is not made by mere human reason, for when the soul makes an assumption it does so because it is sanctified and enlightened by the Spirit of God. It is an instrument in God's hand, for there is the same proportion between the Spirit of God in spiritual things and reason in philosophical things. So as in philosophy, reason makes the major and minor in any syllogism. So also in spiritual things, the Spirit of God enables a man to make a whole syllogism for a believer's comfort and establishment.

How much are they deceived who visibly express the power of sin and Satan in their lives, yet acquit themselves as children of God! Ask yourself, whose image and superscription is this pride? Is it earthliness? Is it hatred of what is good? Though our Savior told the Pharisees they were the children of the devil and did his works, yet they flattered themselves, saying they were the children of Abraham. Does not the apostle say that the works of the flesh are manifest in envying, railings, drunkenness, and other such sins? Yet how bold are men who live in such impieties! Do the sacraments seal these things and say they must be done? Does the Word command them? Did Christ die to make us such people? Oh, what a mad delusion it is to live in lying, swearing, uncleanness, or any other gross wickedness, yet persuade yourself that you are in a good state of grace!

CHAPTER 11

How People Miscarry in
Self-Examination by Signs

I shall now finish my discourse about the signs of grace.
The work that remains is to advise you against approaching those many rocks you may split yourselves upon
when you proceed by signs. For though this method
is both lawful and a duty, as we have already seen, yet
much art and skill is required so that our senses may
truly discern the difference between what is good and
evil. We may miscarry in examining ourselves for signs
in various ways:

Prescribing Signs to Ourselves That Are
Impossible to Attain in This Life

Thus there is Anabaptist and Roman Catholic perfectionism, where people are taught that they must find
such a perfect degree of grace in themselves that no sin
shall be in them, at least for some space of time. It is no
marvel if a soul is perpetually tormented when it seeks
for such a ground of comfort within itself.

In 1 John 3, the apostle says that keeping God's commandments is a sign that we are of the truth. Yet in 1 John 1:8 he says that if we say we have no sin, we deceive ourselves. God's children give themselves many sad wounds if they do not learn to distinguish between the truth and essence of grace, and its degrees. Whereas Scripture says those are blessed who hunger and thirst; in fact, it often describes the godly by their desires and their seeking of God's face.

This error is more evident in those who read books or hear ministers preach about the nature and properties of grace yet are unable to find these marks of grace in such a vigorous and powerful manner in themselves. They ought to know that it is one thing to speak of grace in its definition and nature, and another thing to consider such grace as a subject partakes of it. When ministers of God press a grace upon you, they commonly do so in its abstract nature, that is, in its ideal form. Although such a grace has perfect lineaments and shape, it is much debilitated as it is received in its subject.

On the other hand, some torture themselves by seeing signs of grace in themselves that are not truly signs. Thus, partaking of the sacraments, obeying outward ordinances, showing wisdom in matters of opinion and judgment, and exercising great abilities in religious duties may all be done by someone with an unregenerate heart, as appears in those who said, "Have we not prophesied in thy name?"

The apostle says that neither circumcision nor uncircumcision availed anything, but a new creature. Therefore those who define godliness by these common marks are like Socrates, who described man as like an animal without feathers. At one time Diogenes presented a cock plucked of his feathers and said that, according to Socrates, this was a man. As a man should be defined only by the inherent characteristics of manhood, so must a godly man be noted only by what is true godliness.

There are many signs by which people impute grace and godliness to themselves. However, outward ordinances, a different way of church government, and great inward enlargement are not infallible tokens of such grace. Therefore, to drive people away from false assumptions, I shall in time select some choice false signs and write sermons on them.[1] The false prophets and Antichrist shall come with false signs that are so devious that the very elect may be deceived. Also, the hypocrisy and guile of our own hearts are so exceedingly great that we often mistake our copper graces for gold. Know then that if the signs you see in yourself are not essential ones from which you may truly infer the state of grace, you may have ventured your soul upon uncertain reeds.

---

1. In *Spiritual Refining*, Burgess goes on to expound various true signs of grace in sermons 12–18 and various false signs of grace in sermons 19–33.

Testing Our Graces by a False Touchstone

When the apostle John commands us to examine and prove ourselves, he supposes there is a sure canon and rule by which we may measure and regulate those things we doubt, and this is the Word of God. David calls Scripture a light and lantern to his feet. The apostle Paul commends those teachings that may make us wise unto salvation. Thus, when we are commanded to try the spirits and doctrines of men, we must search Scripture, which is the only star to lead us. The entire edifice of our faith must be cut out of this mountain. Also, from this brook David fetched all the stones he needed to fling at the head of the giant Goliath—symbolizing every heretic.

In matters of doctrine, a man may truly say, "I do not believe it because I do not read it." That is also true of those injunctions by which we are to search and try our hearts, for those who suppose Scripture to be the true standard also believe that whatever is light or faulty may be revealed by Scripture. As God is the beginning or cause of grace, so is God's Word the principle by which we may know what is true grace.

Some men easily persuade themselves that they are in a good state because they judge godliness by the principles of the world and human grounds, but not by Scripture. Yet scriptural godliness is as different from a moral man's godliness as the sun is from a glow worm. Though this insect, which may sometimes resemble a worm, has a little luster on a dark night, it is essentially nothing more than a slimy earth worm. We may say the same of the civil, moral, and refined lives of men who claim to be Christians yet fail to have the power of regeneration in them. Erasmus said of Seneca, "If you look as a heathen upon him, he seems to you to write as if he were a Christian; but if you look upon him as a Christian, he seems to write as a heathen."

Many men appear to be full of honor, righteousness, and justice in their dealings. They have so much sweetness and candor in their spirits that if you were a heathen you would look upon them as divine and holy men. But if you look upon them as a Christian instructed by Scripture, you will soon observe how unacquainted they are with a broken and a contrite heart and how ignorant they are of faith and the inward work of regeneration. Then you will realize that they are only "baptized" heathens. So that you will not throw your soul into a gulf, take up the right rule before you and use it to measure yourselves, for you may be admired and much applauded by others for your goodness and piety (as the Pharisees were), yet be abominable to God.

Using Signs in a Prejudicial Way

We miscarry the truth about signs when we use them in a prejudicial way rather than exercise those direct and immediate acts of faith whereby we receive and apply Christ to our souls. The great work of a Christian is to rest only upon Christ for atonement and reconciliation with God out of a sense and feeling of his own need and spiritual poverty. Scripture requires this faith, for this is the faith whereby we are justified, set up with Christ, and give glory to God.

It often happens that a godly man will dig into his own heart to find grace there while forgetting to exercise applicative acts of faith, and thereby fail to close with Christ. Though the perception of our graces may be of some comfort, Christ Himself ought to be much more comfort to us, for graces are only the handmaids and servants of Christ. They are but tokens from Him, not Himself. A man must not only go out of his sins but also out of his graces unto Christ.

In Philippians 3, the apostle Paul debases all of his own graces so as to be found in Christ. Let not therefore your desire for inherent righteousness make you forget imputed righteousness; that is, do not take the friend of the Bridegroom for the Bridegroom Himself. Failing to do so is without doubt one reason why the people of God are so often in darkness and have no light, for they have no comfortable sign or token of God's love for them so they may stay themselves upon God.

Trusting in God and in Christ when we feel nothing but guilt and destruction in ourselves is the greatest honor we can give to God. Therefore, though living by signs is more comfortable for us, living by faith is a greater honor to God. Hence the life of a godly man is called a life of faith, because though God may many times encourage a believer with sensible evidences, yet He does more frequently call him to combat sense and reason. Do not be unacquainted with this way of relying on Christ in the midst of all darkness, for God many times will cause an eclipse of your signs. Many times you will look into your heart and find no comfort at all. You will see nothing but barrenness, hypocrisy, and sins that make you tremble at yourself. That is when depending upon Christ and His promises becomes your only refuge.

Making the Signs to Be More Than Signs

We fail to see the truth about signs when we make them the grounds and causes of our comfort and hope, thus putting them in Christ's stead. The fear of this has made many strongly oppose the value of signs. However, signs may be rightly composed and used so that we find comfort in signs while simultaneously resting only in Christ. But when we take pride in them or put carnal confidence in them, this woefully wrongs our souls.

Consider how Peter in the name of the apostles professed that they had left all to follow Christ (Mark 10:28). He said that with pride and carnal confidence, thereupon seeming to ask, what other signs did they need? To humble His disciples and keep them low in their own eyes, Jesus taught them a parable that said many that are first shall be last, and many that are last shall be first. You may say this parable teaches us that many that are first in terms of time and zeal of affection to do God's service yet lack the truth of grace and inward humility shall be last, or nothing at all in the kingdom of heaven. Or you may say it teaches that many that are first, or have been exceeding forward and active for God with the truth of grace yet are puffed up with pride and trust in themselves (as was true of the apostles at that time), shall be last, that is, shall have less glory and honor in heaven. No matter which of these expositions you accept, both are sufficient to warn us against pride and self-security, for when we discover God's graces in us, this helps us walk more comfortably and thankfully unto God and does not cause tumors or swellings of pride in ourselves.

Failing to Cast Away Self-Love and Self-Flattery

When we try ourselves by signs, we will deceive ourselves if we fail to cast out two cursed corruptions in us: self-love and self-flattery, for by these we persuade ourselves of grace that does not truly exist in us. Hence Scripture bids us to commune with our hearts and to search and try our ways, for without diligent scrutiny we always shall be strangers to what is in our own souls.

Many people deceive themselves, saying they do repent, they do believe, and they do love God with all their heart, when, alas, they do not know the power of these things upon their own souls. Our heart is by nature a liar; therefore, do not believe it. The Pharisees did not know their own hearts when they prayed, fasted, and gave alms. The Jews did not know their own hearts, either, when they cried, "The temple of the LORD, are these" (Jer. 7:4) and offered many sacrifices.

Knowing our own hearts is a supernatural lesson taught only by the Spirit of God. Self-flattery in this matter damns thousands who do not question their own souls about whether they truly repent of their sin and have love for God. Christ said, "Many are called, but few are chosen," which is true of many who are called by God to enjoy church ordinances and privileges, while few have the works of grace that belong only to the elect. Oh, how this terrible sentence spoken by Christ should make us ask the question again and again, yes, a thousand times, whether we are only called and not chosen, for few are chosen!

The other sinful principle to be ejected from our souls is unbelief and suspicious jealousy regarding ourselves—not giving credit to what we see and feel in our souls, but instead arguing and railing against it. For while a man is unregenerate, he is in love with himself and cannot be brought to loath and dislike himself. We see this in Paul when he was not yet converted. However, when the Spirit of God has thoroughly humbled us and made us see our beastliness and filthiness, we may go to the other extreme of failing to take notice of, and even denying, the work of God upon our hearts. Our hearts were once so deceived that now we do not know how to trust them. Hence the people of God are subject to no temptation as much as this: when they are sincere and upright, they only look at the evil in themselves, not at the good God has wrought in them; whereas it is their duty to also take notice of the good God has vouchsafed to them. How shall they be thankful and acknowledge Him if they are ignorant of this?

Failing to Examine Ourselves in the Right Season

When we are full of dark and black temptations, it is not the right time to examine ourselves, for we are in a fog and unable to view things correctly. While Heman was distracted with God's terrors upon him (Psalm 88), his judgments were eclipsed. And how often did David in difficult situations think that God had forsaken him?

When a mirror is broken into several pieces, it deforms the image of a man's face. And as muddied water is not fit to give the true shape of the face, so the heart that is full of temptations from within and pierced with Satan's injections from without puts the soul into confusion. The incestuous person may truly repent of his sin, yet he takes no comfort in it but is even swallowed up by Satan. During this time the signs within him do not have much effect, nor do God's signs from without. Even the sacraments that are seals of God's love do not persuade him.

Believing That No Signs Will Suffice until They Have Persevered to the End

Though it is true that the good ground differed from the bad ground in that it held out to the end, that is not the principal difference between the two, for this persever-ance flows out of the nature of the good soil. Likewise, though affliction and persecutions revealed the falseness of many who appeared to be good soil in Matthew 13, it does not follow that no one can have assurance until they have come to their journey's end. The Arminians much press this point, saying there is no absolute and peremptory election but upon perseverance in faith and obedience. Hence they join the poet who says that no man is completely happy before his death because prior to this faith may decline and apostatize.

It cannot be denied that the revolt and degen-eration of those who had appeared to be pillars in the church have frightened some Christians into think-ing that, in one day or other, through one temptation or another, they might fall away from the faith. But they should rather believe that if grace has truly been worked in their hearts, God has promised to keep them till the end. We may be assured of perseverance as well as present righteousness, for God, who begins a good work in us, will also preserve it to the end. We also have the gracious promise of God's care from the prophet Isaiah, who says that as He gave us being at first and bore us in His arms, so He will also carry us on to old age itself. What God's grace has planted, He will also water and increase.

Failing to Pray for the Spirit to Enlighten Us While We Search for Signs

The Spirit of God is the efficient cause of the assurance of faith, even as He is in the matter of doctrine. For though a man reads Scripture again and again and persuades himself that all of its authors are diligent in writing arguments for the truth, yet these truths do not move him until the Spirit of God sets them home upon him. It is likewise so of sin; though a man reads warnings over and over again and knows he is guilty of the sins that the Word of God condemns, yet that does not touch his heart and make it bleed until God's Spirit convinces him, and then that conviction becomes an evidence of grace in him. Likewise, though the godly exercises of grace are plentiful and copious in us, our heart is not persuaded of grace until God's Spirit establishes and confirms it in our heart. Do not therefore think that by the strength of your natural light you can attain this certainty.

Thinking We May Not Lay Hold of Christ until We Have the Certainty of Signs

Believers are prone to think that the first work they must do when called to God is to see whether they have true qualifications in themselves, and upon the certainty of this, they may then apply to Christ for justification. That is not what Scripture says, for Christ calls out to the hungry, the thirsty, the loaded, the burdened, and whoever has the need and desire for Him, inviting them to come unto Him. Therefore the certainty that we have true grace is not an antecedent to justifying faith, but a consequent fruit of it.

Hence that received opinion, that faith is a strong persuasion that our sins are pardoned, has justly caused many doubts, for this is not justifying faith, but a fruit of it. Ephesians 3:12 says we may have boldness and access to God through faith, and the apostle says in Galatians 2:20 that "the life which I now live in the flesh I live by the faith of the Son of God, who loved me, and gave himself for me." Paul is saying here that a person is not justified by such belief, but rather is supposed justified and united to Christ by a precedent act of faith.

If therefore a Christian should not come into God's presence or lay hold of a promise till he has this assurance of his inward qualifications, he may be debarred from such all his life. In truth, the soul in such difficulty is like Esther, who trembled to go into the king's presence lest he fail to hold out his scepter of grace. So we must not seek assurance before we lay hold upon Christ; rather, by laying hold of Christ, we may come to be assured. Many times Christ offers the hope to a godly man which he once offered to Peter, saying, "What I do thou knowest not now; but thou shalt know hereafter" (John 13:7).

Failing to Compose Ourselves to Properly Receive the Evidence of Grace

We fail to see the truth about grace when we do not properly prepare ourselves to receive the evidence of grace, for we must not expect that God will assure us whether we desire it or not. By our unbelief and peevishness we may refuse the good consolations offered by the Spirit, for though this sealing of God's Spirit is as efficient from Him as conversion is, yet we may in the former and in the latter resist the Spirit of God. It is a great sin to rebel against God's Spirit, whether in the conviction of sin and duty or as comfort to counteract our doubt and distrust. Yes, the latter is a greater sin, for though the Spirit of God convinces and reproves us, yet its particular operation is to convince us of our adoption, thereby enabling us to call God "Abba, Father." Therefore, when we peevishly refuse the Spirit's work within us, we do in a most eminent manner oppose the Spirit in His greatest glory.

CHAPTER 12

The Duty and Particulars of Assurance

Give diligence to make your calling and election sure.
—2 Peter 1:10

In 2 Peter 1:5, the apostle mentions a chain of grace that every Christian must keep linked together. The elements of this grace are like many flowers which make up a garland that every believer is to wear. He suggests diverse arguments why that is so.

First, so believers will not be barren in the knowledge of Christ. Christianity without such graces is like a fig tree without fruit; it deserves a perpetual curse from Christ. So do not look for leaves or blossoms in a believer, but for fruit.

Second, he who is called a believer but fails to have such graces is blind and cannot see far off. He is like the moles or earth mice, which can see nothing, even when they are in the open light. Or else they are blind because they shut their own eyes. Likewise, wicked men may have knowledge of those objects that may be perceived by the senses, but they cannot discern matters of faith, which are more remote.

Now what the apostle says here about the man who is blind and cannot see afar may seem like a contradiction, for if a person is blind, he cannot see either what is near or far away. Some therefore say that the later words correct what precede them. Thus, to say that he is blind means that he cannot see things that are afar off.

But without straining this text, we may interpret what the apostle says here as this: A person may be absolutely blind in his perception of heavenly things. Though he can see earthly truths that are obvious to his senses, he has no perception about heavenly things. It is sad to consider how many people are eagle-eyed in matters of the world while they are virtually blind moles in heavenly matters.

Third, believers must wear these graces because so many people are guilty of ingratitude. They have forgotten they were purged from their old sins when they first professed their faith in Christ and were baptized. At least sacramentally they were cleansed from their former ways of wickedness. Now they should be grateful for graces that preserve them from further defilements.

Fourth, the purpose of abounding in grace is that we cannot have assurance of our calling or election unless we are fruitful in grace. Knowing that should greatly awaken us, for it behooves us above all things in the world to have some comfort about how our souls stand with God.

The Duty of Assurance

According to our text, our duty is to make our calling and election sure. The graces of God, such as justification, adoption, union with Christ, regeneration and sanctification of our natures, and election, form the basis or foundation of our calling.

But how may we make these things sure? Not in themselves, for the purpose of God stands firm by itself. In 2 Timothy 2:19 the apostle says, "The foundation of God standeth sure." And, "The gifts and calling of God are without repentance," says Romans 11:29. But in respect to ourselves, we may upon good grounds be confirmed in our own hearts that we have truly been called or chosen by God. Therefore, the Holy Spirit does blame here all who put their trust and hopes upon a venture and yet maintain doubts and uncertainties in their own souls about their eternal condition because they will not seek the comfort-producing evidences herein described.

The manner in which this glorious privilege of assurance may be attained, Peter says, is by giving diligence to this matter. We must set our main thoughts and strength upon this matter, for unless we carefully set our souls to distinguish between what is true and false, we shall never upon good grounds be persuaded of our faith.

This text has caused much controversy between Roman Catholics and Protestants. The Roman Catholics deny the certainty of assurance, while Protestants strongly plead for it. This text seems to be an impregnable plea for assurance, affirming that it is not only possible but a duty for Christians to endeavor for the assurance of their effectual calling and election.

We are not to bring an ill report as did the ten spies who gave a report on Canaan, saying such difficulties as giants were in the way so that the land could never be conquered. Like them, some say the assurance or certainty of faith is not only impossible, but it is not even to be desired lest it breed presumption and eat away humility and godly fear. I will not enter into this controversy here. Rather, I will lay down some particulars of assurance, then explain those things that may beget this assurance as well as those effects that do necessarily argue such causes.

The Particulars of Assurance

Let us discuss some of the particulars of this doctrine:

The Necessity of Divine Assistance

When we say that a believer may and ought to be assured of his calling and election, we do not mean that he may attain this divine persuasion entirely by his own efforts. If it were possible, many of God's own children would never have lain in such uncomfortable desertions and dark dungeons as they have done, having no light and crying out that they had no certainty or assurance of faith, that they could not believe or have any comfort, but their hearts were like a barren heath or a black hell.

A believer cannot come to this assurance by himself, for it is a gift of the Spirit of God. Romans 8:16 says, "The Spirit itself beareth witness with our spirit, that we are the children of God." Regarding this passage, sound divines affirmed that assurance lies in a practical syllogism:

+ Whoever believes, repents, is heavenly minded, and is tender about all sin, is certainly called and elected by God.

+ "I am marked by these things," says the gracious heart, enlightened and enabled by God's Spirit.

+ Therefore, "I am called and elected."

The heart that is by nature blind or deceitful could never make such a statement without the help of God's Spirit through the Spirit of adoption. Only by the Spirit may we cry, "Abba, Father." Until God's Spirit evangelizes us and puts a filial frame in us, we remain afraid of God. Our thoughts are slavish and despairing, and we desire to hide ourselves from Him. But the Spirit of adoption calls out our tormenting fears and enlightens our minds so that we may see the good things God

has wrought in us. Hence we are told not to grieve the
Spirit of God, because the Spirit seals us until the day
of redemption (see Eph. 4:30). Thus, as colors are the
object of sight, they are not good or visible without
light; for if there is no light, the eye cannot see colors.
Likewise, even if God has wrought a wonderful change
in you through repentance, you will never know such
excellent graces as assurance in you unless the Spirit of
God enables you to see them.

The Nature of Assurance

The soul of a man, being rational and spiritual, acts in
two ways. First, there are direct acts of the soul whereby
the soul immediately and directly responds to some
object. Second, there are reflex acts of the soul, by which
the soul considers and observes what acts it does. It's as
if the eye is turned inward to see itself. The Apostle John
expresses this fully, saying, "We know that we know"
(1 John 2:3). So, when we believe in God, that is a direct
act of the soul; when we repent of sin because God is
dishonored, that is a direct act; but when we know that
we do believe and that we do repent of our sin, that is a
reflex act. Now whether this certainty or assurance is a
certainty of faith or of sense, or a mixture of both, is not
to be disputed here. To believe, then, is more than probable conjectures and human certainty, which the Roman
Catholics plead for.

The Privilege of Assurance

It is a sin if we do not yearn for assurance or do anything that may justly fill our hearts with doubt and distance. Yet, assurance is not absolutely necessary to salvation, nor is it a necessary effect of our calling and election at all times, as heat is an inseparable effect of fire and light of the sun. We see David and Christ Himself in such spiritual desertions, though there was unbelief in David but not any sin in Christ. Faith of adherence is many times present when the faith of evidence is not. Although it is a great sin to do the things that may grieve the Spirit of God and chase away our assurance, yet many times the people of God may walk without this comfortable persuasion. Yes, they may be greatly assaulted as if God had cast them off forever. They may be like Paul's fellow passengers in the ship, who saw no sun for many days. Let not therefore any argue that they are not called and not elected simply because it has not yet been made sure to them. Many times God works the greatest certainty out of the most perplexing doubts, and the shaking of the soul makes the root falter.

Assurance and Doubt

This assurance to which the apostle presses us is not free of doubts and the oppositions of Satan. As the father of the demoniac cried out, "Lord, I believe; help thou mine unbelief" (Mark 9:24), so we may pray, "Lord, I am assured, yet give me more certainty." When Nathan told

David his sins were forgiven, David still prayed for pardon (see Psalm 51) because guilt and doubts in his soul were working to obscure and darken his faith.

Consequently, in 1 John 3, the apostle John calls assurance the persuasion of the heart. That implies that the heart, being sensible of sin, is full of arguments, questions, and contradictions against God's assuring promises. Hence the scriptural word used most often for *comfort* is also used for exhortation, because to the heart that is grieved and troubled about sin, comfort will not be received except by means of frequent exhortation. Therefore, the opinion that having assurance means being without doubt is much to be suspected as not being of the Spirit of God. For the flesh lusts against the spirit in all its actions, and the devil diligently assaults our comfort and assurance.

If our assurance is of God and is spiritual and heavenly, the heart of a man and the devil will surely oppose it. Presumption, which is the sin of man's self-flattering heart, struggles with no contradictions. The saying of a solid divine is true, which is that none are more desperate than those who, not being partakers of God's grace, are least despairing in themselves.

Assurance and the Work of the Spirit
We will not discuss here whether the Spirit of God does by direct testimony persuade the soul of its good condition and interest in God. Rather, we shall speak of the

mediate assurance that the Spirit of God works in us by arguing from its effects to the cause and from the fruits of grace to the root. This is not subject to such dangerous delusions as the former is, for this is founded upon a sure ground, the fruits of mortification and vivification. The apostle plainly refers to this assurance, for by adding one grace to another and by abounding in the fruits of holiness, believers may make their calling and election sure.

Let us also consider the effects of grace. If a man walks in the ways of grace, he may partake of this privilege. Yet God, by His absolute sovereignty and for holy ends, may leave the most precise and circumspect Christians in darkness, without any light. Job suffered in that way. The prophet Isaiah asked, "Who is among you that feareth the LORD, that obeyeth the voice of his servant, that walketh in darkness, and hath no light?" (Isa. 50:10), thereby suggesting that a person who fears God and is precious to Him may walk in darkness, having no light. All he can do is rest his soul on God by the mere act of recumbence, without any assurance at all. God may ask a believer to live in such darkness, yet if he lives in obedience God may yet give him the white stone promised in Revelation 2:17. He shall walk as one acquitted from his sin, and no one can tell him what he feels but himself only.

How to Obtain Assurance

To obtain assurance of faith, we must do the following.

Give All Diligence and Heed to Obtain This Privilege
We must make it our business to importunately beg for assurance in prayer. We must heed the text to give all diligence and not neglect this duty, no matter what we pass by. It is no wonder that natural men look upon this as a matter not to be regarded, for they have never felt the wounds of sin. They have always embraced self-fullness and self-righteousness, and by this means have not breathed and thirsted after assurance of salvation from sin. It is said that he who never doubts will never learn.

Because he has never experienced the depths of God's displeasure against sin, or His frowns and anger, an unbeliever has never come to think, "Oh what a blessed and happy thing it is to be truly assured of the grace of God and to know that I am such a one to whom the covenant of grace belongs! How wonderful it is to be a child to whom the promise is given, and not a dog!"

People without this privilege do not consider it a great mercy. They do not prize it above all other things because they have never been sensible of the need for it. They have never lain wounded by sin nor were amazed at the hypocrisy and unsoundness of their hearts. They have never felt as if they were dropping into hell, and therefore they have not been diligent to seek this assurance. You see in earthly things how careful men are to make their bargains sure, and in all purchases to make their evidences sure. Poor men think they are undone if they lose their evidences about an earthly inheritance, yet they never think they are miserable if they have no true ground or evidence for their spiritual condition.

Walk as a Fruitful Servant in the Ways of Holiness

Sparks that are ready to go out barely give evidence of a fire. Likewise, we doubt of life when we can scarce feel a person's breath. So it is here. The more remiss, negligent, and lazy we are in the ways of godliness, the less certainty we will have of our salvation. The reason is plain, for if graces are the sign or seal of assurance of faith, then the more these are present and the more thriving and flourishing they are, the surer testimonies they will be of our calling and election.

When the church was lazy and negligent, she lost the comfortable presence and enjoyment of Christ. Standing pools and sluggish waters beget croaking frogs. Likewise, he who prays as if he prays not and believes as if he believes not takes the way to have wounds and blows and all manner of tormenting fears in his heart. Though grace that is exercised is not the cause or merit of your salvation, yet it is an infallible sign of your salvation. It is like the rainbow, which is not the cause but a sign that God will never again drown the world. Hence Paul argues from fervency in grace to assurance, saying in 2 Timothy 4:7–8, "I have fought a good fight…henceforth is laid up for me a crown of righteousness." His Christianity was a real combat with sin, with the world, and with all manner of opposition. He had not been idle or cowardly, but was always upon his watch. As a result, he had a comforting persuasion of his salvation.

Nothing will darken your soul more than dull, lazy, and negligent walking. Abating or decaying in graces will create sad division between God and your soul.

Preserve This Assurance by Walking in Humility and Meekness and Avoiding All Presumption and Self-Righteousness

In Philippians 2:12, the apostle tells us to work out our salvation with fear and trembling. We must do so with exceedingly great humility and debasement of self. True assurance is far from nourishing carnal presumption and sinful confidence, for that is contrary to holy fear and trembling. Though some may be assured of grace in themselves, yet they do not trust this grace. These two things differ as much as heaven and hell.

Paul was certain that nothing could separate him from the love of God (Rom. 8:38–39). He said in Galatians 2:20 that Christ "loved me, and gave himself for me." Yet Paul did not say this because of his own righteousness, but in that of Christ's by faith. The godly may rejoice in testimonies and arguments of grace in themselves, but they put no confidence in them. They repent with holy fear and trembling. They pray and listen to God with holy fear and trembling.

Preserve This Assurance by Tender Watchfulness
against All Known Sin

Sin separates the soul from God and causes a great gulf between them. Therefore, knowingly allowing or willing to sin destroys assurance. Holy certainty is expressly different from carnal presumption, which makes a man confident and bold even though he is in the habit of committing gross sins. Unbelievers can live in uncleanness, in lusts of the flesh, in the contempt and neglect of God and His worship, yet be vehemently persuaded that their hearts are good and that Christ will save them, as if they have committed no sin. Oh, that the way might be made for Christ in them by throwing away all such dangerous conclusions! For as David says, "If I regard iniquity in my heart, the LORD will not hear me" (Ps. 66:18). And the apostle John expressly says in 1 John 3:21, "If our heart condemn us not, then have we confidence toward God."

A believer's heart condemns him for many defects and failings. However, what the apostle is speaking of here is a condemning for the willful practice of known sins. It is no marvel, then, that if you complain you have no assurance, you have no certainty, for as long as your soul desires these desperate ventures into sin, it cannot help but have continual quakings. If Cain carried guilt in his conscience about slaying his brother, it is no wonder that he feared everything would destroy him. David could have no peace in his bones either, as long as any sin lay unconfessed and unforeseen in him.

Take Heed Lest You Grieve the Spirit of God
or Quench His Motions

It is the Spirit of God that witnesses to us of salvation
and the Spirit who seals salvation. To have assurance of
salvation, we must do nothing that may resist or repel
the Spirit that grants it. The Spirit's office is to comfort
and bring gladness to the heart. Now if you rebel against
the motions of the Spirit or by despairing thoughts
reject this Comforter, you will take the sure way to undo
assurance of faith. As you are to hearken to God's Spirit
convicting you of sin and sanctifying your nature, so you
must also receive His sealing and witnessing of God's
love to you. Though the Spirit of God moved upon the
waters at creation and still does upon godly sorrow, yet
this is not the sorrow that is unbelieving, despairing,
and accompanied with hard thoughts of Him.

Acquaint Yourself with the Covenant of the Gospel
and Its Precious Promises, with God's Gracious
Condescensions of Love in Christ

Many children of God are kept in doubt and confusion
because they fail to consider the riches of Christ's grace
revealed in the gospel. They even judge unbelief and
doubting as a kind of duty, as if to do otherwise were
arrogance. Luther said that his soul hated the word *repent*
while he was a Roman Catholic because he thought there
was nothing in it but bitter sorrow and terror about sin.
However, when he understood the evangelical nature of

repentance accompanied by faith in Christ, he realized that nothing was more acceptable to God than believing in Him and having good thoughts of Him as Father. Then that word which he once ran from, as Moses did from the serpent, he took up and embraced.

In conclusion, let us consider how severe must be the reproof of the horrible, profane, and supine negligence of most people in the matter of assurance. Who gives all diligence to make their calling and salvation sure in their own conscience? Who does not venture forth in this matter? Who does not put their trust upon miserable uncertainties? Those who are involved in matters of estate by the law or who are taking medicine for their health, will be careful to proceed upon good ground. Yet in matters of religion they never inquire or seek after the truth. Oh, we would think that religion and a godly fear would make you to know no rest in your bones till you knew what condition your soul is in before God! Have you never heard that the heart is deceitful above all things? The heart will tell you that you have repented when you have not or that you love God when you do not. Will you still glibly put this matter off, saying, "If I will be saved, I will be saved; if damned, I am damned"?

CHAPTER 13

The Assurance of Our Calling Demonstrated, and Answers to Objections

You have heard about the possibility of assurance and of our duty to strive for the certainty of our calling and election. You have also heard about the means by which we may expect this privilege. For a clearer understanding of this, I will now answer one or two objections so that by this discussion the truth may be further revealed, as a file gets off the rust. Since this doctrine contains two elements, the possibility of assurance and the duty of it, we shall question both parts in order.

One of the objections I shall go into here is that such certainty is not possible. This is a most practical objection, for what most usually obstructs assurance in the godly are hypocrisy and deceitfulness in the heart. The Christian who is tender about his condition toward God commonly raises this objection.

The objection is stated like this:

> I know the promises are true and good and without question. He who believes and repents shall be saved. He who is born of God and is effectually

called may conclude, "I am my beloved's, and my beloved is mine." But whether I truly know so or not is my perplexity. Truly, the heart is full of guile. Thus we read about Ahab's humiliation, the failure of the foolish virgins, the stony and thorny ground, those who have some affection and delight in holy things, and some who have sorrow and humiliation about sin yet their hearts deceived them and their gold proved dross. Some thought John the Baptist was the Christ. Some seemed to have perfect dispositions for the complete and effectual workings of grace, yet did not. So why may not I delude myself? Everyone is apt to flatter himself. We see many people who are far from the kingdom of heaven, for between them and godliness is a great gulf. Yet they peremptorily conclude that all is well with them. As Solomon says in Proverbs 21:2, "Every way of a man is right in his own eyes"—and what follows should make all tremble—"but the LORD pondereth the hearts."

In response, this is a very specious argument. Its only strength is the truth that no man should easily and speedily persuade himself that all is well with him and that those duties of searching and trying the heart and communing with oneself privately are to be again and again practiced by us. Yet the doctrine of the hypocrisy and desperate guile of the heart does not overthrow scriptural certainty. Before I give you the reason for that, I shall set down some arguments from Scripture and reason that prove the possibility of such certainty, then answer objections to it. For if Scripture manifests by Scripture that such a thing may be, we may not entertain a thousand objections made to the contrary. Let us go on, now, to offer the grounds for assurance of faith.

The Grounds for Affirming the Possibility of Assurance

Scripture Requires It of Us

God would not require us to search for assurance if it were not possible to obtain it. If our text, "give all diligence to make your calling sure," which seems to speak this truth in the sunbeams spoke of the impossible, might not anyone stand up and say that this commands us to give all diligence to what cannot be? I may as well be asked to touch the heavens with my hands or remove the earth from its center.

Besides this text, I shall cite another impregnable place, which is like a flood pouring from a rock and which all the Roman Catholics have been unable to stop. Second Corinthians 13:5 says, "Examine yourselves, whether ye be in the faith; prove your own selves." As an artisan tries his metal to see whether it is counterfeit or true, so the Greek word for testing here signifies the duty of a Christian to test himself to see whether he has the earnestness and affection that marks true faith. The objective of this duty is to see whether you are in the faith and Christ is in you—that is, whether you have been effectually called or not.

We may also reason from the absurdity that if you do not know that Christ is in you, you are a reprobate. The English word *reprobate* may seem overly harsh here, but the Greek word signifies nothing more than being unskillful in mind or unable to discern. Thus *reprobate* here does not signify one who is not elect, but rather one who is foolish, weak, or unskillful, much as Scripture speaks of reprobate silver (see more of this in the first sermon). So the apostle uses the word here to mean one who is ignorant and weak and unskilled in the ways of God and the works of grace, which he cannot discern in himself. So then let this text put it out of all question, for when the apostle commanded the Corinthians to examine themselves to see if they were in the faith, he would not have done so had that been impossible. It would have been as absurd for them to do so as for a physician to come to a diseased person and tell him he could not be cured unless he ate a phoenix or used the philosopher's stone, which of course cannot be found.

The Spirit of God Seals This to Us

The peculiar office and work of God's Spirit is to witness with our spirits and seal us in faith. The Spirit of adoption subdues the tormenting and slavish fears about God that make the soul suspect everything and be tossed up and down like uncertain waves on the sea

(Eph. 4:14). First Corinthians 2:12 says, "Now we have received, not the spirit of the world, but the spirit which is of God; that we might know the things that are freely given to us of God." The Spirit makes such things clear (1 John 3:24) so that even in the midst of doubt we may appeal to a greater power than our own hearts.

We may also consider what great things the Holy Spirit can do in our souls. No man by nature hates his sin or denies himself; it is the Spirit of God that sanctifies him until he is ready and willing to seek to know the things given to him by God. Nor can any man who feels the horrible depths of wickedness in his own heart be persuaded of such unless the Spirit of God rebukes these waves and temptations and makes all serene and clear in the soul.

Scripture Offers Us Examples of People with Assurance
The people in Scripture who have plainly declared their assurance of faith show us that assurance is possible for the children of God and that therefore we ought to imitate them in it. When in 2 Kings 20:3 Hezekiah says, "Remember now how I have walked before thee in truth and with a perfect heart," he does not say so arrogantly, but humbly, making use of his sincerity as a testimony to confirm him in his prayer to God. Hezekiah could not have used such an argument had he not been assured that he was not deceived in what he uttered to God. Likewise David in his psalms often

professes his love to God with his whole heart and in the uprightness of his heart. That would have been vain bragging and sinful ostentation if David had not known it was true.

In the New Testament Paul often speaks of his assurance and confidence, and, lest it might be thought he had this by immediate revelation, he explains that this is the result of the divine Person who indwells all believers—the Holy Spirit, who witnesses with our spirit (Rom. 8:15–16). Likewise in 1 John 2, the apostle John says we know that we know. He does not make this a peculiar privilege granted to God's favorites, but says it is a mercy that all believers are capable of obtaining. And when our Savior asked certain individuals if they believed with their whole heart, that would have been a vain question which no one could have answered if they could not be certain whether they believed or not. Also, that man who prayed, "Lord, I believe; help thou mine unbelief" (Mark 9:24), showed the certainty he had in the first place of his faith as well as the weakness of it in the latter part of his statement.

Joy and Thankfulness Ought to Be Evident in the People of God

What joy can there be in a soul when it is ignorant or doubtful of God's love? How can the heart be enlarged to praise God for those spiritual mercies which he does not find in itself? Romans 14:17 says the children of God have joy in the Holy Spirit, which 1 Peter 1:8 describes as "joy unspeakable and full of glory."

Can we have this joy while uncertain about our spiritual state? Can we joy in the promise, yet doubt whether it is ours? Can we rejoice in Christ Jesus, yet question whether He died for us? As for praise and thankfulness, how can any man who doubts bless God for translating him out of darkness into light, working the fear of Him in his soul, and effecting the wonderful and mighty change in his heart? Can the soul bless and praise God if he does not think God has done these things for him? Let these thoughts suffice for affirming the possibility of assurance.

The Reason for Assurance

The reason for assurance is that by the supernatural habits or principles of grace, believers may vitally and evidently perceive their actions and effects as rational and animal principles. As love for God and repentance of sin in their acts do manifest themselves spiritually as rational principles, so a rational man knows the arguments and discerns his acts and can tell you that he is of this judgment and not of that. Thus it is with a spiritual man, that he perceives the faith and love of God that are in him.

Can animal love find sensible love burning within? Does not a spiritual lover feel such fire in his bones? Does not David cry out that his soul breathes and longs for God? Does not the church cry out that she is sick with love? So then, supernatural principles acting in the soul are perceived spiritually just as rational or sensible acts are. As Augustine said, he who believes finds that he does believe; in other words, he perceives God's Spirit assuring him. Otherwise, like Hagar, there may be a pleasant foundation of refreshment nearby, yet she fails to perceive it until God opens her eyes.

Why, then, do some people believe such certainty is impossible? Their doubt may arise from three grounds.

1. *They think the effects of grace are not sure signs unless they are perfect and complete.* This deceit appears in good and tender hearts who believe they do not love God enough, are not heavenly minded or zealous enough, are often afflicted with failings, and have daily infirmities. Because they fail to have perfect workings of grace, they doubt any graces at all. But if that is so, then Hezekiah, Paul, and all believers who enjoyed the privilege of assurance should have been stripped of it, for at the same time that they complained about the remainder of their corruptions, they felt thorns and goads in their sides. So it is very important to note the difference between the truth of grace in its essence and its increasing perfection in degrees.

2. *They for the most part keep a remote distance from God.* People who doubt the possibility of assurance often fail to be diligent and constant in their spiritual duties and

approaches to God. Because they do not draw nigh to God, God does not draw nigh to them. Because they are estranged from God, God is estranged from them. If we take Scripture's counsel to walk with God and acquaint ourselves with Him through lively meditation and other quickening duties of religion, we will find that blessings such as assurance of faith, which we thought impossible, are yet possible. The effects of all acts are thought impossible to those that lack the skills to do them. Thus assurance is a mystery and impossibility to those who do not have a familiar acquaintance with God, who fail to come into His presence and do not delight to draw nigh to Him.

3. *They have a servile, slavish fear about God.* People who doubt that assurance is possible nourish a slavish fear about God and do not pray for the Spirit of adoption and a filial, evangelical heart. They may be greatly provoked by aggravated consciences, which are shaken by fear and terror for sin. They fail to distinguish between a fear that arises from a sense of duty and an anxious fear. Many times this is a labyrinth that good people find themselves in. Their hearts are not directed into the way of believing. As the apostle says in 2 Thessalonians 3:5, they fear God as an austere master who is waiting for the opportunity to damn them. They do not have the reverential fear of a father that is accompanied by faith and love of God.

Cain and Judas split their souls upon this rock of terror. Horror had taken hold of them because of their wretched condition due to sin. They had no faith in God as a loving Father, which would have been the thread to help them out of distress. Oh, do not delight in your disposition of bondage. Do not look upon God with slavish fear. This will only reap hatred and blaspheming despair.

Having dispatched these things, let us go on to answer the first objection.

Objection 1: The heart of man is so deceitful that it cannot be assured of faith.

In Psalm 19:13, David says, "Cleanse me from secret sins." There may be a great deal of unknown wickedness in me, such pride, such earthliness, and such unbelief that I never can understand matters of faith, much less assurance of it.

Answers

1. *Though a man may be deceived in his judgment about himself, it does not follow that he is* de facto *always deceived.* We know that general councils may err, yet they did not always *de facto* err. Likewise, a man in judging himself may be deceived at one time or another, but if he were deceived about every act, that would result in such gross skepticism that no man could know his own

thoughts or affections and there could be no such thing as truth in the world.

Scripture speaks to the contrary. First Corinthians 2:11 says, "What man knoweth the things of a man, save the spirit of a man within him?" So a man may know the things of his own spirit. Again, if this objection were true, no man could discern either the content of his faith or his experience of saving faith. No man could tell whether he was a Protestant, Roman Catholic, or Socinian, his heart being too deceitful. I may think I believe such a point, when indeed I do not. This opens the door to such academic doubting that eventually nothing is known and nothing is believed.

2. *Though the heart is by nature deceitful and full of guile and hypocrisy, through conversion and sanctification it is made sincere and upright.* The converted heart is not like those pictures which represent something at a distance in different forms from what is true. Rather, it is like a mirror that honestly represents the form of a person, whether deformed or comely. Nathanael the disciple was said to be a man in whom was no guile. Likewise Psalm 32:2 says, "Blessed is the man unto whom the LORD imputeth not iniquity, and in whose spirit there is no guile." Hence the converted heart may be called an upright heart, a sincere heart, and one that has truth in its inward parts. Although there are residues of guile and hypocrisy and other sins in their hearts, yet in the main the godly are sincere.

Self-flattery and self-love are for the most part crucified. This is the full answer to the objection that the heart of a man is so deceitful that it cannot be assured of faith.

Objection 2: Assurance would tempt us to become carnally confident.

As God keeps the hour of our death and the judgment day from us so that we are always prepared, so He keeps the knowledge of our condition from our eyes that we might always fear Him.

Answers

1. *If the truth about God and Scripture cannot be maintained or asserted by men because their corruption will abuse it, we must preach no divine truth at all.* No good or sound truth produces as its genuine effect anything but what is good. Yet by accident or because of the poisonous disposition in some men, the sweetest flowers may be turned into poison.

Paul frequently preached the grace of God in the gospel, and some of his hearers turned this truth into wantonness. Shall therefore no mention be made of this grace? If some men, through Satan's delusions, think they have grace when they do not, shall not he that has true grace be persuaded of it? If a man in a dream thinks he has riches and honor, should we conclude that the man who is awake can have no certainty about whether or not he is dreaming? Furthermore, by this reasoning no man should earnestly contend for the true doctrine of faith, and no man should inseparably adhere to the truth of God even unto death because a heretic who tenaciously maintains a damnable heresy may be as confident as an orthodox man. We, like the Israelites, should make good use of God's manna, for if we do not, we may find it corrupted by worms.

2. By its very nature, assurance cannot breed arrogance or cause one to neglect God and godliness, for many reasons. First, assurance of faith is only maintained and kept up by humility and holy fear. When a man ceases to be humble or to have a holy fear of God, his certainty likewise ceases, even as a lamp goes out when the oil is taken away. Psalm 25:14 says, "The secret of the LORD is with them that fear him."

Second, assurance cannot breed arrogance because the exercises of grace are only signs and testimonies of election or salvation; they do not cause it or merit it. How then can the soul become puffed up?

Third, the gracious effects of salvation are not of our own working. They are not due to our free will or our natural power. Ephesians 2:10 says, "We are his workmanship, created in Christ Jesus unto good works." Though the discovery of these effects may enlarge the soul much to praise and glorify God, it does not result in stirring up pride in us.

Fourth, these very effects of grace which are not wrought by us are also not yet purely good and perfect. There is much dross and imperfection in them so that while the godly heart rejoices, at the same time it may also debase itself. It rejoices to see the love of God in the soul, but this love is so weak, so languid, and so fainting that it also grieves. It discovers thousands of failings and imperfections and is therefore laid low. Furthermore, though we may have assurance in our hearts, yet in ourselves we do not have eyes to discern what God has wrought for us unless He enables us. Thus it is God's gift to be assured. How many dear children of God walk in darkness and would give the whole world to have this clear evidence of God's love to them, if only for a day!

Application

By means of further exhortation, prove and examine yourselves to see whether those visible characters of grace be in you, or just the marks of the devil. See what fruit you bring forth, for by those signs you may judge whether or not you are trees destined for eternal burning. Oh, it is a sign that all is not well when you are unwilling to examine yourself by the touchstone of truth. It is an argument that there is guilt within you, that you are afraid you may discover yourself to be such a one as you are afraid to think about. You fear that if certainty be only had in the use of such means, then "farewell my hopes, my evidence for heaven." Oh, who says as David, "Search me, O God, and know my heart…and see if there be any wicked way in me" (Ps. 139:23–24).

In addition to the means we have already mentioned, let us add the sign that never fails: we may know we have true faith if we love the brethren and delight in those who are godly, even as David's delight was in the saints of the earth. He that is not godly himself cannot heartily love one who is godly because similitude is both the cause and effect of love. Godliness is the cause of love, not riches, gifts, or reciprocated love. It is simply the holy image of God appearing in him.

CHAPTER 14

Assurance versus Presumption, with Directions to the Godly

The possibility and duty of obtaining assurance have been declared and proved, and the practical objections against them removed. Now let us examine the great advantage of this certainty, where the godly heart has this holy assurance and persuasion worked by God's Spirit. There are many helps that the tempted soul lacks. It is therefore good to propound these helps to you so that the profitableness of it in heaven's way may excite you to seek it.

The Advantages of Assurance for the Godly
Assurance Enflames and Enlarges the Soul to Love God
Against all reason and experience, Roman Catholic theology asserts that assurance of God's love in us breeds contempt, security, and neglect of God. For with all ingenuous natures (and such are the children of God), the more persuaded one is of another's love, the more

love is repaid with love. The more a wife and child know they are beloved of husband and father, the more they are enflamed to return that love.

Love is fire, and fire turns all things into fire. When David knew that God had forgiven his iniquities and healed his diseases, he said, "Bless the LORD, O my soul: and all that is within me, bless his holy name" (Ps. 103:1). Likewise, in Romans 8:6, what put the apostle Paul into ecstatic raptures and transcendent expressions about God and Christ but the assurance that he was elect, called, and justified by God?

Oh, know that you will struggle with doubts and servile fears as long as your love to God is imperfect and cold, for the fear of God brings hatred and wearisome thoughts of Him. Hence the apostle in 1 John 4:18 says that slavish fear has torment within it, and only love can cast out such tormenting fear. Love for God as a gracious Father would allay such tempers within us and calm the swelling waves that are in our soul. That cannot be done unless we have some certainty that God loves us. When we know that God is pacified, our soul is also pacified. As the sea is quiet when the air and wind above are quiet, so the soul is calm, comfortable, and gracious when it by assurance may enjoy God's favor. If we cannot vigorously love God without this certainty, we should be provoked to strive more vigorously after it.

Assurance Breeds Spiritual Strength

Certainty of our calling and election breeds much strength and heavenly ability to perform all graces and duties in holiness with lively vigor. Fear, by contrast, makes our hands weak and our knees feeble. It disheartens us, as if a lion were in our way. By contrast, the certainty of our good condition puts hope and life into us. The testimony of a good conscience made Paul active in the course of his ministry (cf. 2 Cor. 1:12). And as Nehemiah 8:10 says, certainty breeds joy, and the joy of the Lord is our strength.

If a piece of timber is full of moths and worms, it is not strong enough to support a building. Likewise, grief is rottenness in the bones, which consumes the heart of our strength. Spiritual dejection and sinful doubts about the work of grace in us consume our hearts and destroy their very foundations. No one but a sanctified person can have a good conscience in a scriptural sense without assurance of faith. A person may have a quiet conscience that does not accuse him of gross sins committed against the light of nature. But that is not a scriptural conscience, for that belongs only to one who is freed not only from gross sin but also heart sins and soul sins and is sprinkled with the blood of Christ.

Thus we must continually seek a good conscience; such a conscience is like a good feast. This will stir us to seek holy certainty, for with it we will be far more cheerful and more joyful in the work of the Lord. We will be more fervent and zealous, for we will be as the sun or a giant running a race. We may complain of our barrenness, our weakness, and our sloth, but what can give us wings besides the certainty of our gracious state? It is like the spirit in Ezekiel's wheels or the wind that gathered dry bones together. Oh, that the people of God would be more concerned about this matter, for they are like a mere lump of earth spiritually if this breath of life is not breathed into them!

Assurance Supports the Heart during Afflictions and Outward Miseries

Had Paul not been assured of that eternal weight of glory, he could not have judged the worldly miseries he suffered as light and easy. When David was in misery with all his outward hopes gone, he encouraged himself by saying that God was his God (1 Sam. 30:6). He knew that God was his God even though he had lost everything else.

The apostle Paul said he was more than a conqueror because of this assurance. He could challenge all troubles to hurt him, because he knew by God's Spirit that he was called and chosen to do His work. Shall not this same yearning prevail with you? Is it not miserable to fear being killed by men and damned by God at the same time, to be imprisoned by men and at the same time be imprisoned in your own conscience? Oh, what will provoke you to seek assurance if not this?

We are sure of nothing—not of life, outward comforts, nor of outward enjoyment. Will we not, then, be sure of grace within? Oh, when will we be wise? We vainly labor for earthly things that cannot give us everlasting assurance when we should be yearning for grace. So many people are like bees, which all summer long have labored to fill their combs with honey. Then the husbandman comes along, burns the hives, and takes the honey. So, too, do you labor long to gain much wealth and property, only to have death, or a sudden public judgment, or war come upon you, taking everything from you. When we cannot be sure of any outward thing we have, let us be sure of inward grace.

Assurance Protects Us against Temptations and Assaults

The certainty of grace is a strong and mighty buckler against the violent assaults and temptations that the devil uses against the godly. Satan tempts the godly into believing that they are hypocrites. He also tries to persuade them that God is bringing calamities upon them because He is not reconciled with them and because they seek themselves and not the glory of God.

There is no stronger wall to repel the devil's darts than the testimony and knowledge of the truth of grace in our hearts. That was the water of life which sustained Job in the midst of his fiery temptations, when God seemed to be fully against him and godly friends judged him a hypocrite. The devil assaulted this good man by questioning his motivation, saying, "Does Job serve God for naught? God hedges him in, and gives him outward prosperity. No wonder then that Job serves the Lord." These were such strong, tempestuous winds of doubt that they might have torn up the root of the strongest oak, yet Job stood strong because he was sure of his integrity and sincerity. He knew his aims and ends were pure and that he served God for God's sake.

As the certainty of grace defends us against the devil's accusations, it also protects us against the calamities and thrusts of the devil's instruments. As the devil is the accuser, so wicked men also charge the godly with hypocrisy, calling them dissemblers and painted sepulchers. Yet the godly who are assured of their own uprightness and the graces of God in their soul are abundantly fortified, whereas it is terrible for those who are accused by other men as well as their own consciences, feeling condemned by men and by God.

Assurance Brings Contentment of Mind and a Thankful, Cheerful Heart in Every Condition

As we have already said, David encouraged himself by knowing that God was his God. In many psalms, David says the Lord is his portion and his inheritance. He could not know this unless he was certain of his godliness, for God is not the portion or inheritance of wicked men. Because of this assurance, God put more joy into

David's heart than those whose wine and oil increase (see Psalm 4). If you would have happiness on earth and true contentment of spirit, it must come out of the knowledge of God's love for you in Christ. You may then say, "Soul, take your spiritual ease and be quiet, for many good things are stored up for you." This is to be a godly rich man; indeed, rich in soul, and to fare deliciously, in a spiritual sense, every day.

Assurance Is an Antidote against the Fear of Death
The certainty of grace is a sure and special antidote against death and all fears of it. It makes the king of terrors a king of all consolations, for seeing that by grace we are members of Christ, death has no more sting for us than for Christ our Head. Thus the godly in Christ may say in triumph, "O death, where is thy sting? O grave, where is thy victory?" (1 Cor. 15:55).

We may handle the serpents of death because their stings have been removed. Those who howl and roar at the approach of death do not know whether God is their friend or enemy. They have just cause to think He is their enemy and that they may be going to hell rather than heaven. The very name and thought of death and judgment strikes their souls with astonishment and terror. But those who are in a holy manner persuaded of their interest in Christ and who perceive the sure evidences of God's grace in themselves may lift up their heads even as death draws nigh, for their redemption is sure.

This should much incite you to seek such support for the hour of death. When the sentence of death was passed on him, Hezekiah supported himself with this assurance (2 Kings 20:3). What will you do when the hour of death approaches and you are without the comfort of your riches, wife, and children and no longer have the company of your friends and acquaintances? When you are no longer sure of any earthly comfort, would it not be better to be sure of heavenly comfort? Oh, be wise for your latter end. Do something that may steady you when you are dying and gasping for breath, for drowning men will reach out for anything to save them. Dying and drowning men should be sure of a fast hold to lean upon. These are some of the advantages of the certainty of grace.

The Difference between Assurance and Presumption

The godly heart may inquire, How may I distinguish between holy certainty and persuasion by God's Spirit, and my own persuasion arising from the self-flattery in me? Do not thousands of people call darkness light, and bitter sweet, and conclude they have the truth and goodness in their hearts in all respects toward God?

It is true there are foolish dreamers who dream of their fullness when they are indeed empty. Yet to a searching eye those dreams may be easily distinguished from what is true.

The Difference Is Evident in How We Live

Holy certainty is maintained by the exercises of grace and the constant, tender avoiding of all known sin, while presumption assumes God's favor despite obvious sin. A presumptuous person is confident of God's love and of his own good heart, yet at the same time he may be notorious for various sins, such as taking God's name in vain, constant lying, being unjust in his dealings, and living by the flesh in lust and sensuality. Oh, such people must be beetles to live in the dung of such presumption, but they are certainly not Christ's doves, who humbly delight to dwell in the sweet places of obedience. How can you hope in God, saying you have a good heart and conscience, when you have such wickedness in your life? This is impudent presumption, and God's eyes are too pure to accept or love such. A man who truly has grace in his heart takes great care to practice good duties and to avoid all known sin.

Presumption Is Unwilling to Be Searched and Tried

A person who presumes to have assurance of faith flees from the light of examination. It cannot abide being tried by the touchstone of faith. By contrast, holy certainty loves to be deeply searched. The difference between a heretic and an orthodox man is that a heretic is anti-scriptural, as Tertullian said. He is like a bat or owl that flees from the light. Likewise, a thief hates the light, says our Savior in John 3:20. But the truly orthodox person desires to be tried deep within his soul. A person with the true knowledge of grace cries out with David in Psalm 26:2: "Examine me, O LORD, and prove me; try my reins and my heart." A person without presumption would not try to bring a false title or forged evidence before a judge to argue his innocence.

Presumption Does Not Bear Up under Calamity

Presumptuous confidence in one's salvation may prevail for a time, but when great and extraordinary calamities occur, this bubble bursts and vanishes away. This confidence is not truly rooted and therefore cannot abide a violent storm. Such a man falls from presumption into despair.

By contrast, see how Job and David fought through the hardest thickets filled with briars, yet these innocent sheep did not lose their wool. Likewise, dross will melt in the fire, but gold will be more refined. The wind makes chaff fly away, but the wheat prevails and is more purified. So the righteous has hope in his death, says Proverbs 14:32, while the presumptuous man's hope most often withers.

Presumption Is Not Opposed or Assaulted by the Devil

Satan does not tempt the presumptuous and labor to drive presumers out of their false confidence. Rather, he nourishes them in it. The devil only targets those who have a holy certainty of faith in order to drive it from them. Satan was not afraid to shoot his fiery darts even at Christ, to tempt Him to doubt whether He was the Son of God. Likewise, the devil's strategy was to make Job think he was a hypocrite and condemn himself for it.

Godly assurance is much opposed both by the devil and the unbelieving heart of man. It is hard to obtain and hard to retain. But of presumption we may say, as Isaac did of the counterfeit venison given to him by Esau, "How is it that thou hast found it so quickly, my son?" (Gen. 27:20). Likewise, we might ask a presumptuous one, "How came you to be so quickly and easily confident of faith? How could this man-child be born so quickly, without the pangs and sorrow of childbirth?" That is not God's way.

Presumption Divides the Means from the End

Presumption hopes for the privileges of faith, though it wills not to perform the duties of faith. But this is not genuine assurance. It is a presumptuous delusion, for our text tells us to give all diligence to make our calling sure.

Presumption is like the man of false charity that James speaks of, who says good words to people in need, then bids them to go home and be warmed and clothed but does not give anything—which is the way most people live. Presumption hopes for a good end but does not talk about the means to that end. Presumptuous men would not tempt God by denying their sinful nature, for all men would say that was a horrible presumption; but they will palpably act so with regard to supernatural life by neither repenting of sin nor forsaking its ways or striving after holiness. Yet they hope Christ will be their Savior. Men do not see their own folly and madness in these matters.

Presumption Is about Self-Deception

A man deceives himself with the false logic of presumption, whereas true certainty is a knowledge wrought only by the work of God's Spirit in us. The apostle James says, "If any man among you seem to be religious and bridleth not his tongue, but deceiveth his own heart, this man's religion is vain" (1:26). Such a man makes a false syllogism (indeed, all presumption is a false syllogism), taking that for a cause what is not a cause. Or else he is ignorant of the proper state of the question: "What does it take to be truly godly?" for that question goes to the true nature of assurance.

Presumption Takes Pride in Self while Condemning and Undervaluing Others

The Pharisee was guilty of such arrogance when he prayed, "God, I thank thee that I am not as other men." By contrast, true assurance is accompanied by deep humility and a profound respect for others, praying and mourning for them, saying, "Oh, that their eyes were opened so they might be enriched with the grace of God!" Humility and selflessness are inseparable effects of godly assurance and are precious in the sight of God. The most humble thoughts we have of ourselves are as great as doing the greatest and most excellent things.

How a Godly Man May Have Assurance

What should the godly person do when he has grace but lacks assurance? Though grace is in him, he does not know it, but thinks the opposite. In Luke 24:16, the resurrected Christ appeared to His disciples. Though He drew near to them and talked to them, yet our text says, "Their eyes were holden that they should not know him." So with many a gracious heart, Christ may be spiritually present in the soul. Grace may even be present, yet the person cannot feel it. Though the Son of Righteousness is in his heart, he walks in darkness.

Continue to Depend upon God

To such a one we say, let him walk in a faith of adherence and dependence upon God even if he is not sure of these evidences. This is what Scripture calls trusting, rolling, leaning, and staying the soul upon God. David in many of his psalms says that he only has this plank to stand upon in the great ocean. Though assurance is a duty, and we must press after it, it is not what justifies us. You may belong to God and have an interest in His promises even though you feel no evidence of it. Isaiah 50:10 says, "Who is among you that feareth the LORD, that obeyeth the voice of his servant, that walketh in darkness, and hath no light? let him trust in the name of the LORD, and stay upon his God." So if you see your soul as a parched land, a withered branch, or a dried tree, consider what God requires of you. This dependence of faith is far more noble than assurance of faith.

We should continue to exercise holy duties and love God because of the sensible sweetness and delight they bring, but also because in dependence we learn to trust God even more when we have no sense or feeling of that. As it is a greater act of love to God to love Him even when He afflicts us or blesses us with no outward mercies, so it is a greater act of obedience to wait and depend on God when we feel our own unworthiness and load of sin than when the goodness of our heart is cleared up to us.

Trust That Depending upon God Will Strengthen Your Faith

To depend and wait on God, though darkness is in your soul, will make your faith more firm and strong. When the woman of Canaan continued to beg Christ to heal her daughter even when Christ called her a dog, it only increased her faith. Likewise Job, in the midst of great sorrow and suffering, cried, "Though he slay me, yet I will trust in him" (Job 13:15). So do not fail to be constant in your holy duties, and do not become discouraged in waiting on God for assurance. In due time He will cause the sun to rise and the dark night to fly away.

In conclusion, let me press you to be upon sure and certain terms about your souls. God told Hezekiah to set his house in order before he died. Oh, set your soul in order and reconcile all your spiritual accounts. It is a woeful thing to cry out when you are dying, "Oh, I know not what to do. I cannot live, but I dare not die, for everything is in disorder within me, and there is nothing sure about my soul."

What do you think, dear friend? Is this not the greatest reason in the world to be diligent about such matters? How inexcusable will you be on that day? How can you go away and say, "It is true, indeed, that we should be upon sure terms with our souls before God. It is a happy thing to be so. But the world and my lusts hinder me from doing so."

I tell you, the consideration of these matters so affected men in the past that they lived in cells and holds of the earth and shut themselves up in woods and wildernesses so they might attend to this great matter of the salvation of their souls. That, indeed, was their purpose, even though many operated out of blind zeal and indiscreet forwardness. You must be diligent to seek assurance of faith, for at the Judgment Day your failure to do so will rise up and condemn your jollity and carnal security.